Curt Iles
God is faithful!

The Old House
Front Porch Stories

Curt Iles

ISBN: 1-4033-5226-7 (e-book)
ISBN: 1-4033-5227-5 (Paperback)

This book is printed on acid free paper.

1stBooks - rev. 09/04/02

The Old House
Front Porch Stories

Front cover: The front porch of the Old House, Dry Creek, Louisiana

Back cover: "Doten at the Old House" Painting by Bill Iles. Theodosia Wagnon Iles, or "Doten" as she was called by her family, lived at the Old House in Dry Creek from when it was built in 1892 until her death in 1964.

Acknowledgments

So many people have encouraged my writing that there is no way to properly thank every person who has aided me. A special thanks to all of you who encouraged me to step out and publish these stories from my heart.

I've been fortunate to have many helpers and proofreaders, especially the ladies in our camp office and Jill Aguillard, Kimberly Crider, Amanda Lafitte and Mark Weldon. I also appreciate the willingness of all three of my sons, Clay, Clint, and Terry in allowing their lives to be shared through many of these stories.

Finally, thanks to my sweet wife and favorite reviewer, DeDe. I'd rather hear her say, "I really enjoyed your story" than to receive any glowing book review or fleeting moment of fame.

Introduction: The Shortest Road to London...

Many years ago, the London Times held a contest. The rules of this contest were relatively simple. The winner would be the person who could fill in the following sentence with the best ending:

The shortest road to London is ____________.

Many creative ideas were sent in. However, the winning entry was both simple and deeply profound. Here is what the insightful winner of this contest wrote:

The shortest way to London is **with good company**.

How true it is that any journey is a pleasure while traveling with good friends. This is especially true in the journey of life.

The book you are holding is simply a journal written about many of the companions who have journeyed along with me. Some of them are from the distant past, while others walk along beside me now. They all share one thing in common- these are folks who have been both wonderful traveling companions and enlightening teachers for me. My sincere wish is that this small book, written from my heart, will be good company as you take it on this stage of your journey.

As we travel together for these next few miles and days, please remember that I am simply one of many fellow strugglers, walking along together, as we try to understand the twists and turns of the road called life. As you join me for these simple stories of the joys, sorrow, humor, and beauty of life, my sincere wish is that these stories will awaken your heartbeat of discovery, and help you focus on the things that really matter in this life.

Happy traveling,

Curt Iles
Summer 2002

TABLE OF CONTENTS

Dedication

Specifically I would like to dedicate this book to my parents, the most wonderful couple I know. All through my life, when I've met people and they found out who I was, they'd always smile while saying, "Oh, so you're Mary and Clayton's son." When they said that, I knew I was at least starting off with a good reputation. It was up to me not to mess it up from there. To my wonderful mom and dad, I personally say this: Thank you for teaching me the value of family, love, friendship, and caring. Thank you for showing me, by your lives, what followers of Jesus should look like. Thanks for giving me a good name.

"A good name is more desirable than great riches."

Proverbs 22:1

The Old House at the End of the Road

If it's possible to love a house like a person,
Then the Lord knows I love this old house.
It's a place reminding me of family,
And the things in life that really mean the most.
It's a place I return to when I'm lonely. . .
. . . Or it seems I've lost my way.
A place where I always feel welcome,
As I sit down and think for a while.
This old house is more than boards and nails
Because it tells me of our past . . .
As I walk through it, I'm reminded that
The special people in our lives never last.
Although they're gone, I will remember
How they still live on inside of me.
Because this old house reminds me of who I am,
And everything I ever want to be . . .

There it sits- surrounded on the east side by tall long leaf pines and along the west fence line by oak and hickory trees as the land slopes down to the swamp. Out in front is a dilapidated old barn, and behind this house to the south are overgrown fields- once bearing tall field corn and purple hull peas, but now grown up in a tangle of briars, tallow trees, and weeds.

In the middle of this sits the most special place on earth to me- The Old House. Built by my great-great grandfather in 1892 on land he and his wife homesteaded, it is now vacant, and slowly deteriorating the way homes do when not lived in. However, to me it is a beautiful place of peace, reflection, and solitude. As the above poem states, it is the place where I go to get my bearings and remember what is really important to me.

Recently, my sister frantically called me at work. "A woods fire is burning close to the Old House!" I ran to my truck and quickly drove to the Old House which is next to the home of my parents. As I turned down their gravel road, I could see the dark smoke billowing up above the tree line. The one-mile drive down the road seemed much longer as I hurriedly drove, wondering how close the fire was to the most special house I know. I've always lived with the fear that the Old House would burn.

I sped by the homes of my parents and two sisters, and parked in the driveway of the Old House. I breathed a sigh of relief seeing that the fire was much further away than my sister, Claudia had thought. I was both relieved and thankful.

As I sat in my truck looking at this original log house, built onto by five generations of my family, I was once again reminded why this is my favorite place in the entire world. I've gone far away over the years but invariably I return, in body and spirit, to the Old House at the end of the road.

You see, the Old House is where I come to write. On a beautiful spring day like today, when the world is once again alive with the dazzling greens of early spring mixed with the colors of the azaleas, dogwoods, and honeysuckle, my heart yearns to sit here and write.

On days like today, I write on the porch, sitting in the same rocking chair that "Pa," my great-grandfather, sat in as he read Louis L'Amour books during the last years of his life. It's the same porch where his son, my grandfather, would call up to our house, two hundred yards away, "Come on down. I've got a fresh pot of coffee." Out front is the same yard where he would yell out his "pig call" each evening and woods hogs would come tearing out of the swamp for the shelled corn they knew awaited them.

During the chill of winter it is often too uncomfortable to sit on the porch, so I move inside to the middle bedroom.

There by the double fireplace, I attempt to stay warm by sitting right up near the fire and doing what I love best-writing.

There's an art, which I've never quite mastered, of being up close to a fireplace without getting too hot. The trick is to get warm and toasty on the front of your body, while your backside is freezing to death. The most important thing is to remember is not to let your front side get too hot. Nothing burns worse than the front of your jeans sticking to your legs as you move away from the hot fire.

During these cold days of winter, my fingers become numb as I type on the laptop, but I still love being here. The warmth and companionship of a fire, whether it is a blazing campfire in the Arkansas mountains, or this fireplace, gives comfort and security to anyone fortunate to sit beside its warmth.

Often, when I've camped in the woods, it has amazed me how a campfire unites a group of men- physically as they huddle together, and emotionally as they begin to open up. Something about staring into a fire causes us to lose our inhibitions- somewhat like being under the influence of alcohol. I've seen tight-lipped men, who normally would never show outward emotion, gaze into the fire, and begin telling their deepest secrets. The eyes of a man staring into a campfire as he shares deep feelings from his heart, is a scene not easily forgotten. As this man talks, the warm reflection of the fire in his tear-filled eyes create a reverence in those of us as we listen.

It seems a good fire has the same effect on my writing. Stories seem to just appear and burst forth, as I stare into the December fire and hear the cold wind moaning through the cedars in the front yard. Sitting here, I'm accompanied by the popping and crackling fire. From time to time, a hot ember pops out of the fireplace against the fire screen. In the same way, ideas for stories just seem to be conceived and spring forth as I sit bundled up in this room.

This middle bedroom is where some of my older ancestors died and where others in my family were born. It's the same cozy room where I always best loved to sit and visit with my grandmother. It was peaceful as we would sit there visiting, just rocking back and forth.

Sitting here today, there are still two rocking chairs by the fireplace. The one next to where I'm sitting is empty now. My, what I would give to spend another evening rocking and visiting with Mama in front of this fireplace.

When I sit bundled up by this fire in the middle bedroom, I know a telephone is not going to ring for two reasons: First, there is no telephone in the old house which is just fine with me. Secondly, my cell phone won't work here deep in the woods. A cold day at this old house with no ringing phone is worth the frozen toes and numb fingers. This room becomes my hideout. I can well understand this quote from Susan Allen Toth:

"A closed door, a comfortable chair, a view out a window-maybe that's all that a hideout requires."

However, true winter days are rare in Southwest Louisiana, so most of my writing times are on the front porch. The outside sounds of nature motivate me just as winter's fireplace flames. Pausing from writing, a nearby red cardinal flies by as a reminder to write about him. A green lizard scurries by on the porch railing, stops, and puffs up the red sac under his neck. As he "shows us his money," I laugh at the absurdity of this great ego in a two-ounce body. Just like me, mister lizard thinks he is the king of all he surveys, when in fact we are both just travelers passing through and enjoying the pleasure of being here on the front porch.

All of these gifts of God through nature prompt future stories to be written. There's something about sitting on a porch in the woods, alone and silent, that causes a peace to settle in my soul, and the ideas for stories just seem to naturally come to the surface.

So from the front porch of this log house, in the edge of Crooked Bayou swamp, is a good place to begin this book. A book of simple stories of the people of six generations who've lived, laughed, cried, and died here. A book of stories about the lives, experiences, and special people of my community. A collection of stories from my heart, written in the setting of a place I love: The Old House . . . at the end of the road

A *Prophet* has no Honor in Dry Creek

This story is nearly too good to be true, but it actually is. The funniest things in life are not fictitious, but real events that take place all around us.

My next-door neighbors in Dry Creek are Mark and Mitzi Foreman. The Foremans, and their two children, Mavy and Mark, Jr. operate Foreman's meat market at the intersection of Highways 113 and 394.

This story is not meant to be a commercial, but if you've never eaten boudin or sausage from Foreman's, you haven't lived. They are known far and wide for their wonderful Cajun-seasoned meats. My son, Clint, loves to get his mom's shopping list and add, "Buy plenty of Foreman's sausage." Famous all over our area also are their huge stuffed pork chops and chicken breasts. These delicacies, filled with boudin or sausage, are a feast by themselves. You can also get a greasy paper bag full of fresh fried cracklings, which are authentic crunchy pork skins.

The Foreman's opened their Dry Creek store in 1993. They've been very successful due to a great location, a quality product, and lots of hard work. Mark and Mitzi are talented business owners and deserve every bit of the success they've had.

However, this story is not about them. It's about their son, Mark, Jr., better known in Dry Creek as "Boom Boom." For the sake of simplicity, I'll call him Mark, but if you come in Foreman's Grocery, ask for "Boom Boom."

Mark Jr. is a businessman and sausage expert just like his dad. Presently, his responsibility is making cracklings at the store. He can also discuss, in detail, the fine points of red pepper, casings, and correct sausage cooking times. My boys sat with him on the school bus and loved to relate how he constantly sketched out notebook drawings of improved sausage making equipment. I predict Mark will one day be rich and famous as an entrepreneur, far beyond the confines of Dry Creek.

This specific story happened when Mark was about ten years old. At this age he began attending Catechism, which are the lessons where Catholic doctrine is taught. The very first lesson, from the Old Testament, told about the early patriarchs of the Bible. As the teacher introduced the stories of Moses, Abraham, and Isaiah, she asked this question, "Do any of you know what a prophet is?"

The children looked at each other waiting to see who'd answer first. However, they shouldn't have waited, because Mark Foreman already knew the answer and was excitedly waving his hand back and forth.

The teacher asked, "Mark, tell us what a prophet is?"

Without any hesitation, Mark replied,"A *prophet* is the money you have left over in your business, after you've paid all of your bills."

Fully satisfied with his excellent answer, this future business tycoon sat down. I'm not sure if he passed Introduction to the Old Testament, but I'll bet you a bag of hot cracklings he'll pass Economics 101.

The Sign Phantom

It all began in the spring of 1974, just prior to my graduation from high school. A rainy April had kept the local streams flooded in "Dry Creek." (The world's most overworked cliché, "Well, how wet is it in Dry Creek?")

One afternoon I went down to the green "Dry Creek" sign that informs the northbound traveler that they are entering our community. Over the "Dry" in Dry Creek I taped a white poster board sign saying "Wet." It now read, "Wet Creek." It was widely noticed and laughed at by everyone.

The Lake Charles American Press even ran a picture of the sign, in a story commenting on our wet spring. The caption read in part, "The Highway Department is looking for the 'wag' that placed this sign, in defiance of regulations prohibiting the defacing of public signs." This kind of caused me to lay low on my sign authorship. But for some reason, everyone in Dry Creek knew I'd done it.

Shortly after that, I placed another sign. This sign (to appease my humor-challenged highway department friends) was tied by hay string to the signposts below the Dry Creek sign. It read:

Fun City, U.S.A.

This sign was meant as a final tribute to my soon to be former home as the prodigal left "the sticks" for bigger and better things in college. To understand this sign, you must know something about Dry Creek- both the stream and the community.

To some, the name Dry Creek conjures up a small community in southwestern Louisiana. Others think of the church camp of the same name that has been in existence there for over seventy-five years. Then, some folks think of one of our three churches or two crossroads stores.

The creek called Dry Creek is a small, muddy, steep-banked stream that meanders through the southeast corner of Beauregard Parish. It is not very wide, deep, or pretty. It was first named by the Indians. One old timer related as to how he'd been told the Indians really called it "Beautiful Creek," but the English translation got messed up and came out as "Dry Creek." Others claim the more traditional story of its name coming from the fact that the creek dries up in places in very dry weather.

Then, there is the geographical area known as Dry Creek. To call the community of Dry Creek a "town" is a gross exaggeration. Nestled among pine uplands and hardwood creek bottoms, Dry Creek is simply an intersection of two highways. We have a post office, a church camp, two stores, and some really good churches, but very little in the way of commerce or industry.

This still happens to me from time to time: A first time visitor will stand in the Post Office parking lot and innocently ask, "Now, where is the actual community of Dry Creek located?" It's always fun to answer with a smile, "Friend, you're now standing right in the middle of downtown."

Not much exciting has ever happened exciting in our community. Growing up I only remember two really big events- Once, when a crop-dusting airplane crash-landed on the highway, and the other when the post office was robbed. Therefore, to call Dry Creek, "Fun City, U.S.A." was to make light of what most anyone would agree is a quiet and boring community.

Later during the fall of 1974, I returned home from college, and was informed that "my signs" had continued to appear. My pleas of innocence were met with knowing smiles and winks. According to local folks, these signs had continued to appear at the same location poking fun at our community with such gems as:

"Hee Haw Filmed Here,"
"Airport Next Exit,"
and
"Famous for Nothing."

Even though no one believed my repeated denials, I had a good idea who the real sign phantom was. Later that year on another visit home, I saw a new sign and both the humor and handwriting gave it away. This sign related to the predicted "swine flu" epidemic that was of grave concern in 1975. Doctors were advising many people, especially the elderly to receive vaccines. This new sign read: "We ain't gonna give our hogs no flu shots."

I immediately knew my father was the sign phantom. My dad, a lifetime highway department worker and church deacon, reluctantly admitted to me that he had continued the sign tradition. In the coming months when I would be home, he would enlist my help accompanying him to help put up his signs.

I'd always know, even without seeing him, when he was preparing a sign by the sound from the back room, of him laughing softly as the squeaking of the magic marker announced a new sign was on the way.

We'd leave out late at night to put up the signs. His signs at this time continued on their themes of small town life and country values such as:

"Shop our Modern Mall,"

"It Sure Ain't Heaven,"
and
"Toll Bridge- One Mile Ahead."

Our longtime postmaster, Kat King, told of a stranger stopping at the post office for directions on how to avoid the toll bridge. A female driver wanted to know how to get to the nearby mall.

The signs continued and the legend of the Sign Phantom grew. I was still the number one suspect and no manner of denying could stop folks from believing it. All of my alibis about my being away from Dry Creek were not believed. At that time, I don't believe anyone even suspected my quiet and respectable dad.

Even though our community is small, many travelers pass through Dry Creek on their way to DeRidder or Bundick Lake. The story of the signs at the Dry Creek bridge began to spread throughout southwest Louisiana. Folks would stop in at the store to comment on the signs, and even complain about their absence, if no sign was up.

(Some signs, especially those controversial, never stayed up very long. Any sign commenting on hunting, religion, or Edwin Edwards, were quickly ripped down.) But this never bothered the Sign Phantom of Dry Creek, who never seemed to have writers' block or run out of new ideas.

One lady from Westlake, who traveled our way weekly to her fishing camp, sent a letter addressed to the Dry Creek Chamber of Commerce. For anyone to think we had a Chamber of Commerce really tickled us. Her letter had many questions about the signs. She said that each week her entire family began leaning forward in their seats to see what the latest sign said. She listed these as her favorites:

"We Have a Fine Sense of Rumor,"

"Crossroads to Nowhere,"
and
"First Annual Fire Ant Festival Next Week."

Many times the Sign Phantom commented on current events:

"Wedding Saturday Night Baptist Church- Bo and Hope" (From the soap opera *Days of our Lives*),
"Herb Lives in Dry Creek" (From the famous Burger King Ad series)
"Killer Bees- Death Awaits You Here" (As the dreaded killer bees approached Texas)
and
"Protected by Patriot Missiles" (During Operation Desert Storm).

Additional social comments were made on signs such as:

Gun control- "Our wives, maybe. Our guns, never!"
The lottery- "Waiting for the lottery to make us all rich."
Hunting- "Do not shoot squirrels that wave or smile at you."
And even professional wrestling-
"Don't tell us that wrestling is fake!"

One of my personal favorites concerned an event that took place about fifteen years ago. Up in a bay in Washington State, three whales were trapped and could not swim out due to the shallow water at the bay entrance. For several weeks, the national news media kept Americans informed as the plight of the whales. Volunteers from groups such as Greenpeace, stayed at the bay attempting to help the whales.

That same week, a new sign appeared in Dry Creek:

"Help save the three gar trapped in Bundick Lake."

Through the years people never believed it was my dad making these signs. I eventually began answering all inquiries with the plain truth, "It's my daddy doing them, not me." Usually they just laughed as if I was the world's greatest liar.

All in all, the hundreds of signs that were posted at the bridge were a commentary about our world during the 70s and 80s... and Dry Creek's (or more specifically, my dad's) reaction to it.

Some of the signs were not understood by Dry Creek natives. The meaning of a sign in 1990 was questioned by one older resident. "Clayton," this man asked my dad, "What does that sign 'We Dance with Coyotes' mean?'" Evidently, he hadn't been to the movies in a while, and didn't even know who Kevin Costner was.

As I think of the many signs over the years, I recall my all time favorite. It can best be appreciated by an outsider driving through our community:

"Don't laugh. Your daughter may marry a Dry Creek Boy"

I bet my mother-in-law up in north Louisiana, and many other parents who've lost a daughter to a Dry Creek boy, can really appreciate that sign penned by the Sign Phantom of Dry Creek.

Sometimes during the early 1990's, the Highway Department came and moved the Dry Creek sign away from the bridge and closer to the community. They placed it right across from Turner's Grocery. That is when Daddy quit putting up his signs. He said the resident's dogs barked too much when he went to this new location at night. However, the legend of the Sign Phantom still lives on in the community of Dry Creek, Louisiana, also known as "Fun City, USA."

The Wash Spot on Crooked Bayou

The darkness always comes more quickly down in the swamp. I'm always amazed to come out of the dark woods at dusk using a flashlight, and then upon entering the open fields, realize there is still a good deal of daylight left. Deep down in the woods the evening shadows rapidly spread through the swamp. When you are alone, there is no darkness quite like the lonely night that fills Crooked Bayou swamp at dusk, especially if you are there alone.

This particular evening I'm not alone in the swamp. I'm sitting, with my youngest son Terry, on the bank of Crooked Bayou. It is the first day of February, and this is our last squirrel hunt of the season. We sit with our backs against a large oak, squinting through the gathering darkness for any sign of a cat squirrel jumping from limb to limb. The trees are completely leafless, a sign that the depths of winter are here. As I look around at the bare and desolate woods of winter, I recall a story my dad, who is a better writer than I am, once wrote about this time of winter in the swamp. Here are his words:

I went into the woods the last hour of today. I said I was hog hunting, but I really went to recall the strange, maybe eerie feeling that the last day of hunting season used to give me. Something about the barren stark form of trees that have changed so rapidly from the greens, red, and golds of October and November, speak of the passing of pleasures- Pleasures of the crisp smell of early autumn and all of the Saturday morning hunts. Now the tall trees stand naked against the gray sky with a few old weather-beaten deserted squirrel nests hanging precariously to their branches. Gone are the acorns, hickory nuts, and beech mast for another year. The swamp has taken on an entirely new and very somber personality- the silence of impending night settles so easily with only robins in the distance and gusts of wind whipping and whistling through the bare limbs to remind you that it is now deep winter.

As I think about dad's story, the cold winds send a shiver through me. I'm not really sure I even want to shoot a squirrel today anyway. I'm like him in the fact that I've come to see the swamp in the grayness of winter. It's hard to say the desolate woods are beautiful during the bareness of winter, but there is an attractiveness that is hard to describe.

I'm also glad to have an excuse to be in the woods with my son. I've picked this spot, for Terry and me to sit along the creek, for a purpose. We're not sitting here because it is the best squirrel hunting spot. No, I've picked it because this is the old wash spot. Down in the black water of Crooked Bayou, I see four old fence posts sticking up and am reminded why this is such a special place for my family.

This particular bend in the creek was pointed out to me by my dad as where his great-grandparents washed clothes in the days before electricity and washing machines. Looking into the nasty stagnant water, I wonder how they ever washed clothes in that water. Then I recall stories of how this bayou once ran clear and free flowing when the underground water table was much higher than it is now. I remember stories of how they floated logs down this creek and caught fish of all types. That's hard to imagine as I look into the dark water.

Then I recall the stories of my dad's mother, my precious Grandma Pearl. In her memoirs, she described wash day at this very spot, as carried out by her grandparents-in-law, John and Sarah Wagnon, and their daughters, Theodosia and Louise:

Wash day was always a picnic day. Uncle John took the drudgery out of this hard day's work by making it an event that involved everyone in the family. They would take the clothes down to Crooked Bayou where the water ran swift and clear. There was a log across the bayou that Uncle John had smoothed the top off of. On the near bank of the bayou sat a large cast iron pot.

First, the clothes were put in the iron pot and boiled with homemade lye soap made by Aunt Sarah during hog-butchering time. There was much care taken during the boiling of the clothes, so the soap was always stirred by only one person or it might ruin the soap. This was usually the job of Louise. After the clothes were boiled in the cast iron pot, they were taken on wooden paddles, like canoe paddles, and paddled first on one side, then the other, in the cold clear creek water by Uncle John. This rinsing process was done for each article of clothing.

On these days Aunt Sarah would pack a picnic lunch, to be shared by the family on the bank of Crooked Bayou. If blackberries or huckleberries were in season, they were gathered by the bucketful, for when ripe, they were plenteous along the creek.

Today you can still see the place where the family gathered on wash days. A few pickets remain at that crook in the bayou, protruding from the brackish water, giving little evidence of the once clear stream that coursed through these banks and served the family well on wash day.

All of these thoughts come back to me as Terry and I sit in the gathering darkness, right where the iron wash pot once sat. I think of my great-great grandparents, John and Sarah Wagnon, and how I would love to have known them. I recall stories of their younger daughter, my Aunt Lou, who died just before I was born. I relish the seven years I knew their other daughter, my great-grandmother Theodosia, or as we called her, "Doten."

Terry snuggles closer to me, and I know he is ready to go back to civilization, lights, and a warm house. The cold wind picks up in the towering pines, beeches, and oaks. I strain to hear a far off sound.

Above us, I hear the sound of a distant jet flying over. From its sound and direction, I surmise it is beginning its long descent into Houston, one hundred-fifty miles to the west. I try to imagine this planeload of passengers cruising along at thirty-thousand feet. Looking out their windows, they can see the lights of southwestern Louisiana coming on one by one. These passengers, probably mostly city folk who've never sat in the woods at dusk, would think we are pretty strange. Little do they know, or probably care, that down here in the darkness of Crooked Bayou swamp sit two people- a father and son. One is ready to go home, and the other is wishing he could just stay and sleep right here tonight in the swamp against this oak.

Then I wonder at how strange my ancestors, Grandpa and Grandma Wagnon, would find our lifestyle. They'd be amazed that this airplane, six miles high, could safely land humans in Houston, in the same amount of time it took me to walk out of the woods and drive to my home five miles away.

The sound of the jet fades away, and the moaning wind begins its song once again. Nearby a lone owl hoots. Once again, I strain to hear a sound that seems to resemble music. My mind goes back to being a small child and accompanying my dad hunting. Many times at dusk, as I wished for the comforts of home and my mom's supper, I'd hear what I called, "woods music." Across the swamp I'd swear I could hear the sounds of far off music. I never told my dad this because I was afraid he'd make fun of me. In my fertile imagination these sounds could be coming from Indians, elves, or some strange swamp creature.

I smile as I recall woods music, and wonder if Terry hears it right now. I lean my head back against the beech tree . . . and faintly hear it . . . the clear crystal ring of an old country fiddle playing a lonesome mountain ballad.

There's nothing more haunting than a slow and mournful fiddle song.

In my mind I see her- my great-grandmother- as I remember her in the later years of her life. She tucks the old fiddle under her aged chin, shuts her eyes, and slowly begins to play. It seems she is a thousand miles away as she slowly sways to this sad song. There are no words to this song because lyrics aren't needed. The mournful notes tell of lost love, lost dreams, and the pain of loneliness. This song came across the Atlantic from Scotland or Ireland. This same song came down through the highlands of the Appalachian Mountains southward. It came with my ancestors from Georgia and down the Natchez Trace, across the Mississippi, the Red, and the Calcasieu rivers. Finally this song settled here along Crooked Bayou, where it became part of my family.

It's a fiddle tune Doten was taught by her parents, who had earlier been taught it by theirs

I shake my head. The sound of the wind dies down and so does the song. I look down into the water at the four pickets that mark the old washing spot. One last time I see my great grandmother. But this time she is standing across the creek and is no longer the older woman of my childhood, but is once again the young child I never knew- laughing, playing, and singing on wash day on Crooked Bayou. She wrestles with her sister Louise and splashes water on her mother. There is simplicity and peace to the scene as the four of them just enjoy being together.

Then, suddenly I'm awakened by the sound of splashing in the creek. Terry has thrown a stick in the water. This is his polite way of telling me he's ready to go. I quickly notice it is much darker now. Because of the darkness, we'll need to carefully feel our way along toward the Old House. I regret not bringing a flashlight. We pick up our guns and begin the trek out of the swamp. I tell Terry to lead us, and with his good sense of direction, he correctly points out the way toward our truck.

After walking a while, we begin to see the lights of my parent's home- the house where I grew up. As always, it looks so inviting after being in the dark woods. We step quicker now, sure of our destination and direction. One last time, I turn to look back toward the swamp. All I can see is darkness, but through the tall trees I hear the wind blowing softly, and one last time I believe I hear the sound of fiddle music - right back there at the old wash spot on Crooked Bayou.

A Bridge Built on Catfish

Driving over the small bridge across Mill Bayou, I'm filled with disgust at the trash strewn in the ditch. Scattered paper cups, empty bottles, and Styrofoam food containers are everywhere. The anger swells in me and is directed at the highway workers who left behind this trash. This crew, who are working on this bridge, left it behind from their day yesterday. The idea of people having no more pride in leaving a place better than they found it really infuriates me. I think, "Tomorrow I'm going to stop by here and give them a talk about this trash."

Later that evening, I tell my good friend, De'Wayne Bailey, about the highway workers' trash. De'Wayne also works for the Department of Transportation. He listens and then says, "Why don't you just pick it up and leave the bags of trash there? They'll get the message, and I bet they won't leave any more trash."

I follow De'Wayne's common sense idea and pick up three bags of trash. I pile them by the bridge railing and leave another empty bag tied to the railing. I pass the next morning and the ten men are working at the bridge. Passing them, I give a half-hearted wave.

At the church camp where I work, we've just had our monthly catfish lunch. It so happens that we had some catfish, hush puppies, and baked potatoes left over. An idea hits me and I drive back to the bridge to seek out the job foreman. He eyes me cautiously as I approach. I'm sure he is used to being chewed out and hearing every type of complaint imaginable. I simply ask, "Would y'all like to come eat lunch with us today? We've got some leftover catfish." He looks suspiciously at me, and then quickly says, "Yes."

So at lunchtime, they file one by one into our dining hall. I mean no disrespect when I say they were a rough-looking crew. These are men who've worked hard outdoors all their life. Observing them as a group, I see a really good cross-section of southwestern Louisiana- strong rednecks with bulging tattoo-covered biceps, a black man in a cowboy hat, and Cajuns with the unmistakable accent of South Louisiana. They shyly stand at the dining hall door not quite knowing what to do. The men of our staff shake their hands and welcome them, and then we ask the blessing and dig in.

There are a few foods that are just as good when heated up the second time, and fried catfish is definitely one of them. All of us go down the serving line and load our plates. Several of these bridge-builders look as if they have enough on their plate to test the weight limit on the new bridge they are building!

We all sit together at one long table. Initially everyone is pretty quiet- partly, due to our full mouths and partly due to no one knowing what to say. The only sound is the clinking of silverware as catfish meets hungry mouths.

Then something happens to break the awkward silence- I ask one man where he is from. As he tells me his hometown, it so happens I know someone from there, and from that another conversation starts. One of our staff members, Mickey Parsley, who really loves people, begins a conversation at the other end of the table. Soon there is laughter and plenty of good stories from both our staff and these men.

Most of them get up and go back for another load of catfish. They all comment on how good the meal is. You can feel the warm fellowship building in us that is always a magical part of the Dining Hall at Dry Creek Camp. As we finish the meal, the foreman makes a statement that will always stick with me. He looks me in the eye and says, "This is the first time our crew has ever had anyone do something nice for us."

His statement astounds me, but also humbles me as I think of how close I was to stopping on the road and giving this man a royal chewing. Instead, because of God's grace and the good advice of a friend, these men are now our new friends. The simple act of inviting them to share a leftover meal with us has opened the door of friendship.

Then I realize that the relationship we are building with these men is being built on catfish. The meal we've shared with them is the medium through which we've started the process called friendship.

Before leaving the Dining Hall, the men all thank us. Then, Bro. Mickey, who is a true man of prayer, asks them if there is anything we can pray for them about. They are silent, but as he prays God's blessings and safety on each man, their jobs, and their families, I hear several sniffles. After the prayer there is a look in the eyes of those men that I'll never forget.

That afternoon they are still working when I cross the bridge going home. Recognizing my truck, they all wave heartily. We are now friends because of that "bridge built on catfish."

Driving past the waving highway workers, I recall another instance when I saw God use the "fellowship of food" to unite a group and make them feel welcome...

A few years ago, a group of inmates from nearby Phelps Correctional Center came to pick up trash along the highway in the Dry Creek area. Our agreement was for the camp to provide lunch for the twenty men and their guards.

Rea Tate, our cook at the time, prepared a wonderful country lunch- roast, sweet potatoes, turnip greens, cabbage, hot cornbread, and peach cobbler topped with ice cream. Mrs. Rea could cook anything, but her specialty was what we call "soul food." She'd grown up in the Mississippi Delta country and knew the art of simple things cooked in heavenly ways.

At lunchtime, the inmates marched into the dining hall accompanied by the guards. You should have seen their faces when they saw the layout of food. The buffet line itself was a sight to behold.

Awaiting them were pots of steaming vegetables and sliced roast next to pans of cornbread and hot rolls. These men ate and ate, and then somehow found room for more. Rea hovered over them like the big-hearted grandma she is and made sure no one lacked any item. As they ate, I thought to myself, "They won't be able to bend over this afternoon and pick up any trash. They'll be too full of greens and cornbread."

As the men finally finished, one elderly inmate sought out Mrs. Rea. He was an older black man with graying hair. Clad in his faded jeans and blue work shirt, he approached Mrs. Rea in a respectful manner and said, "Ma'am, that was the best meal I've had since June 23, 1974."

. . . And his face showed he meant it. Once again, I'd seen the wonderful power of fellowship that occurs when folks sit down and share a meal together.

Passing the bridge and nearing my driveway, I recall one additional story about "relationship bridges" built on food:

About ten years ago our cemetery board of directors was dealing with a difficult and thorny matter. We planned to meet early on a Saturday morning at the cemetery pavilion to discuss this potentially divisive issue. Starting to the meeting, I was filled with a feeling of uneasiness. I knew this morning could possibly hold disagreement and hurt feelings among our nine-member board.

Before driving to the cemetery, I stopped by the camp kitchen and begged the ladies for a pan of their hot homemade biscuits. I added a jar of homemade jelly, and then picked up a cold gallon of milk and coffeepot. It was a beautiful morning– the type of morning that always makes you glad you got up early. The special spot, here in the edge of the woods where we were meeting, only added to the peaceful atmosphere.

By the time the men started arriving, the smell of freshly brewed coffee wafted across the cemetery. It didn't take long for the men to begin devouring those homemade biscuits. Our Dry Creek Camp biscuits are famous far and wide, and never taste better than when enjoyed outdoors with homemade mayhaw jelly. Everyone enjoyed the food, drink, and the good accompanying fellowship.

The subsequent meeting went well. There was a spirit of openness and sharing that resulted in a decision acceptable to everyone. I believe this fine spirit was a reflection of the wonderful men who sat there together. However, I also believe it was partly due to the fine biscuits and coffee we'd enjoyed together. *Once again, a bridge had been built on good food.*

Over and over, I've seen this principle of relationships work. It's hard not to like someone with whom you've just sat and shared a good meal. I once read a statement illustrating our job as followers of Jesus. It read, *"Building a bridge of friendship on which Jesus can walk into the hearts of others."*

That is our job and calling- building relationships and friendships so we can both share and show others the love of Jesus. . . Moreover, I've seen this bridge best built when its foundation is a meal shared together, whether it is catfish, turnip greens, or fresh homemade biscuits.

Needless to say, the bridge crew never threw down another piece of trash. Each day they would wave enthusiastically whenever I'd pass. Finally, they finished the bridge and moved on. But even now, two years later, some of them will drop in at the camp when they are in our area.

Pray One for Another

...And pray one for another
James 5:16

The power of prayer is strong. The more I learn in my life and from others around me, the more I believe in the awesome power of God that is unleashed when we pray. Over and over, I've seen God do what can only be described as miracles in the lives of people- whether at the camp, through our church, or in the event of our everyday lives. Some folks would call these events, "coincidences," but I'm convinced it's due to God's people praying diligently that He acts in such unique ways.

Through the ministry of Dry Creek Camp, we have a large group, mostly senior adults, who faithfully pray for our ministry daily. They, and many other praying friends, are the keys to what God is doing here on a daily basis.

A big part of our prayer life should be what is called intercessory prayer. Very simply, intercessory prayer is praying to God for people and their needs. Formerly, I was often guilty of making this statement to folks experiencing tragedy, tough times, or trials, "Well, all I can do is pray for you."

I've since learned that the greatest thing we can do is pray. This wonderful quote from Henri Noewen says it much better than I ever could:

"There is nothing we can do better than praying by name to God for others. Nothing unleashes the power of God like the prayer of His people."

Or as Christian writer, S. D. Gordon, shares, "*The greatest thing anyone can do for God and man is pray. It is not the only thing; but it is the chief thing. The great people of the earth today are the people who pray. I do not mean those who talk about prayer; nor those who say they believe in prayer; nor yet those who can explain about prayer; but I mean those people who take time to pray.*

One of my favorite stories concerning prayer is told by my special friend, Della Mercer. She faithfully taught the preschoolers at our church for years. Once at the end of a lesson on prayer, she wanted to finish the lesson by having the children pray. Della stated to the five-year-old class, who were sitting in a circle,

"Now, we are going to go around the circle and pray for each other."

Her plan was to let the child on her right begin and allow each child around the circle to utter a short "sentence prayer."

The first child to her right was Charlie Taylor. Instead of sitting in his chair and saying a short prayer, he got up and began going to each child seated in the circle. As he would put his hand on each of their shoulders, he then prayed with, and for, each child.

As Della watched in amusement, Charlie "went around the circle" praying for each one by name. Della said it was the most beautiful illustration of caring and praying she'd ever seen. Charlie physically did what we should be doing: going to others, showing them we care by putting put a hand on their shoulder, and praying with them.

God has taught me, and is continuing to teach me, a great deal about this. So often folks come to us and say, "Will you pray for me about something?" As they share their burden, we promise to pray for them. However, if we aren't careful, in the midst of our busy lives, we tend to forget about them and their problem or needs.

God has convicted me about this - What I am learning to do is to simply stop right there and pray with them. This ministers to them and God always honors heart-felt prayer. I'll never forget once meeting a Dry Creek neighbor in front of the post office. As we made small talk, this rough-edged man, who seemingly had no room for God in his life, began sharing the heartache he'd recently experienced with a rebellious teenage daughter. His hardened, weathered face showed the pain he was dealing with. The windows to the soul, his eyes, were filled with tears. I did the only thing I knew to do, I said, "Do you mind if we just pray together right here?"

He said, "I wish you would." So there in the post office parking lot, as people came and went, we stood beside his beat up old truck and prayed. He wept openly and even my voice was choked.

I'll never forget the look on his tear-streaked face when we finished. He simply said, "Thank you so much" and slowly got in his truck. That parking lot encounter was the beginning of my journey of praying with people. It really doesn't matter the location, or even if we are on the phone, or when it is, God both hears and honors prayer.

My challenge to myself, and to you, is let God use us as an active intercessory "pray-er." Hurting people are always waiting to know someone cares. They are waiting to hear the good news that God loves them and He can forgive them through the sacrifice of Jesus Christ.

And the fire for God that is waiting to begin burning in their heart can be lit by a single "match" of intercessory prayer from you. Let's follow Charlie Taylor's example by getting up, going to others, showing them we care, and most importantly- praying with, and for, them.

"...and pray one for another."

James 5:16

The Evergreen Cedar Tree

I was born in a small town.
And I can breathe in a small town.
Gonna die in a small town,
That's probably where they'll bury me.
- John Mellencamp, "Small Town"

Driving through the fog of an October morning, it is hard to see very far down the narrow paved road. My truck windshield fights a losing battle with the Louisiana fog and humidity. As I near my destination, Dry Creek Cemetery, I can barely make out figures walking in the cemetery amidst the thick fog, but I know Mr. Leonard Spears is out there.

Today is the second Sunday in October, which is always an important day in Dry Creek. On this date the annual Dry Creek Cemetery memorial service is held. Hundreds of people will travel from as far away as California or Florida to be present for this special day. Today, I'll see folks whom I only see once a year when they return on this day to their Dry Creek roots. However, most of those here today will be like me- country people who've never flown far from the nest in Beauregard and Allen Parish.

Of all the people who will make this a special occasion, there is no one this day means more to than Leonard Spears. Here's why:

Dry Creek Cemetery was originally called Spears Cemetery. The land on which our cemetery now sits was owned by Mr. Leonard Spears' grandfather, Leonard "Len" Daniel Spears. This plot of land, located near the forks of two streams, Bundick Creek and Dry Creek, became a cemetery through a long ago heart-breaking event linked with an act of kindness.

During the nineteenth century, the settlement of Dry Creek was on the main road used by many early settlers as they traveled between the cities of Lake Charles and Alexandria. About twenty years after the Civil War ended, a migrant family headed west to Texas, stopped their wagon in our area due to a very sick young daughter. While camped here, this child died. Mr. Len Spears went to this family and offered to let them bury her in a corner of his field. Because no permanent headstone was available, a small cedar tree was planted by the wooden grave marker. That old and gnarled tree, now over a century old, still stands today in the center of what is today called Dry Creek Cemetery.

The grave of this pioneer child became the first of many, in what originally became known as Spears Cemetery. It soon became the primary burial spot in our community. Years later, its name was changed to Dry Creek Cemetery[1].

It is a special and sacred place for those who have buried the bodies of loved ones here. Just last week some volunteers at the camp from Minnesota drove to the cemetery. Upon returning, they told me, "I've never seen a more well-kept cemetery than the one in your community."

So on this October morning, it is with pride and deep reverence that I approach the cemetery. In the fog, I can barely make out the farthest tombstones and the background of pines and oaks beyond the south fence line. Through this mist, I can barely make out the huge cedar tree standing among the oldest graves in the cemetery. Its limbs are now twisted and the bark shows the signs of surviving years of storms and weather extremes. Yet, despite the toll of the years, it stands nobly as a silent reminder of a rich history.

This big cedar tree seems to be saying, "I've been here a long time and I've seen a great deal. Yes, I've lost many limbs and may look decrepit, but I'm still standing."

In the South, most old cemeteries have a cedar tree growing in the area near where the earliest graves are. The early settlers, very familiar with death, would plant a cedar tree to symbolize everlasting life. With its year round green needles, the cedar tree bore stark testimony to the belief of life after death.

---

[1] Historical information from *History of Dry Creek Cemetery* by Juanita Miller Brumley

This cedar at Dry Creek Cemetery has survived the changing seasons, droughts, storms, and sits in the middle of an increasing number of surrounding tombstones. It serves as a reminder to each visitor here of how death is not the end- death is only the end of life as we know it. This tree seemed to be saying, "Look at me. Look at my evergreen needles. What you are looking at around you, these graves, are not the end, but only the beginning."

About two years ago, a fast-moving spring storm blew through our community. The strongest winds were in the cemetery area, where numerous large trees were blown down. Someone called and said that one of the largest limbs on the old cedar had broken off and fell right on about a dozen old graves.

In mind I imagined broken headstones all over that area of the cemetery. Arriving, I was shocked at how large the broken limb was. On the upper trunk of the cedar, you could see where it had broken off. The loss of the large limb left the tree looking lopsided. As reported, it had fallen right on a large number of tombstones.

To our amazement, not one marker was broken by this huge twenty-foot long limb. Several headstones were pushed over, but none were broken. If was as if the old tree had carefully lay down its lost limb among the graves.

Within a week, the limb had been cut up and the area cleaned. The only reminder of what had occurred was the fresh wound down the cedar's trunk.There was some talk of cutting down the tree before other limbs fell. However, our cemetery board decided to leave the tree as it was for now.

Today, on memorial day, as I stand under the cedar and look around at the hundreds of graves in every direction, I'm so glad the old cedar was given a reprieve from the chainsaw. I know one day it will fall and the cemetery will seem bare without it, but its demise will once again be a reminder of the temporary nature of our lives.

I'm reminded of how our former pastor, Logan Skiles, referred to cemeteries as "the city of the dead." As I look at the markers of various sizes, heights, and ages, it really does resemble a city. There are passageways like streets, and the markers from a distance line up like the tall buildings of a large city.

My primary job at the cemetery is to help families pick out their gravesites. It is both a labor of love and a ministry for me. It is humbling and sobering to stand with a family as they grieve and make final plans on the resting place of a loved one. Thinking of this, my mind immediately goes back to my friend, Arlean.

Arlean is ten years older than I am. We grew up together in Dry Creek. Arlean's grandmother, Aunt Annie Mercer, cooked in the camp kitchen during my young teenage years. Aunt Annie took me under her wing and just loved on me, and for that I will always be grateful.

Arlean and her husband, Jerry, live just down the road from my house. They are my neighbors and friends. One day, Arlean phoned me with the call I'd been dreading. She was ready to go to the cemetery and pick out her spot.

So on this day, I found myself standing with Arlean in Dry Creek Cemetery. But we aren't alone- Jerry is with his wife. Also present was their daughter Dana and Arlean's pride and joy, her granddaughter, Olivia. Arlean's parents, Arthur and Annie Mae Crow, stood to the side as we gathered in the southeast corner of the cemetery.

Arlean had battled cancer enduring a long and heroic fight. She had inspired everyone as we saw how tough, resilient, and positive she had been in this fight. She was aided in this by her family, church, and her deep faith in God.

Standing there today, we all make small talk, but everyone knows the reason we are here. One by one, each family member points out their requested spot as I record it in the record book. Annie Mae Crow wants to be placed next to her mother, and the rest of the family selects spots close by. Arlean walks to the place where her baby, who died in childbirth, is buried. She tenderly stands near that small tombstone and simply points to this spot beside her child.

As we silently stand there, it's evident this trip has exhausted Arlean, so the Crow and Courmier families get in their vehicles to leave. I walk over the truck window and look into Arlean's eyes. There is a look of peace in her eyes that says more than words could ever describe. I put my hand on her hand and we smile. To me, this is one of those moments where reverent quietness speaks loudest. Words are not appropriate, nor needed, right now.

Everyone waves as four generations of the Crow family drive back to their homes. I am left alone among the hundreds of surrounding tombstones- each one a silent and mute testimony to the life of a human.

Two weeks later Arlean died at home with dignity and peace. The next day I met the gravediggers at the cemetery and pointed out the spot for Arlean's burial. Her funeral, held two days later at our church, was a beautiful celebration of her life and love of family. I chose not to go to the cemetery for her burial later that afternoon. I knew the recent time we had spent there together was much more important.

A week later, I went to the cemetery. The first thing I noticed as I walked to Arlean's spot was not the flowers, or the fresh dirt on her grave, or the nearby graves of my beloved grandparents, or the even the open area where I will one day be laid to rest, but my gaze was fixed on something else. My eyes were riveted to only one thing there in the cemetery- the bright green limbs of a stately old evergreen cedar tree, standing proudly in the middle of Dry Creek Cemetery.

First Swim of the Summer

All three of my boys stand with me on the bank of Bundick Creek. It's late May and time for our first swim of the summer. The creek is up and muddy from rain earlier in the week. Clay, Clint, and I all three know how cold the water will be this early in the season. Terry, three years at this time, doesn't know it yet, but he will soon experience it first-hand.

I call the older boys over to join Terry and me. "Guys, we need to pray and ask the Lord to bless our swimming this year." As I put my arms around their shoulders, I pray, "Lord, bless our swimming this year and keep us safe. Amen."

With my "amen," I shove all three of them into the cold water. They come up hollering and yelling, and I know another year of creek swimming has begun. Quickly, while my courage is up, I jump in with them. The icy water takes my breath away and I think to myself, "This is absolutely crazy!"

The boys and I swim as often as possible during this summer. Many times we will go to the large camp pool with its clear water and smooth bottom, but the best place to swim is right here in Bundick Creek at Morrow Bridge. It is the spot where I, and now my boys, learned to swim. There is just something about the smell of creek water, the feel of the current, and the soft slimy creek bottom sand between your toes, that stays in your soul long after you are home and dry.

Trying to get used to the cold creek water, I recall stories about Web Boggs. Web grew up in the edge of Ouiska Chitto swamp near Sugartown. On every day in his life, up to when he went off to fight in World War II, he took a swim in Ouiska Chitto River. His family told me that regardless of the temperature or weather, he faithfully took his daily swim in the creek. One of his sisters told of how one night at bedtime, Web realized he'd not had his daily swim, so he got out of bed, put back on his clothes, and went down to the creek for a moonlit swim.

Later as I sit in the sand, watching the boys splash and play, I think of how many children never experience the uniqueness of swimming in a creek, or the exhilaration of swinging off a rope tied to a limb high above the water, or just soaking in the changing light and quiet tranquility of enjoying a sunset sitting on the creek bank.

Because my boys are growing up so quickly, I know the day will come when going to the creek with their dad will not be "cool" and I'll be begging them to go, instead of them begging me. I recall the wise words of Stephen Covey in his book, *First Things First*. Covey states,

"I've never heard of a man on his deathbed expressing regrets that he didn't spend more time at the office. But many times men have been at the door of death and lamented the fact that they wished they'd spent more time with their precious family."

How sad it is when a person, standing in the doorway as they watch a teenager leave home for good, regrets not seizing more of those special moments that fill a parent's heart. So, I'm thankful to have another summer of swimming in the cold water of Bundick Creek. I know that sometimes this summer when I'm busy with chores or paperwork, one of the boys will come to me and say, "Daddy, do we have time to go swimming today?" I'll think of all the tractor bush hogging needing to be done, or how the bills need to be paid, but I hope I'll reply with the "swimming daddy's" motto: "Boys, I can think of a lot of things we need to do besides going swimming. However, right at the moment, I can't think of anything more important. So, let's go."

Ten Years down the Road...

It's been a decade since I wrote the swimming story above. My, my how time flows by so swiftly. Today is Christmas Eve, always one of my favorite days of the year. It's been a cold but beautiful clear day.

My day has been happily busy with wrapping presents, getting ready to barbecue ribs tonight, and working on my writing. I am in the last stages of finalizing the manuscript for the very book you are now holding. It needs to be at the publishers soon and I'm trying to squeeze in every moment I can to write, edit, and re-write these stories.

After being out in the backfield for a short break, I'm headed back inside to my laptop for some more book work. Clint, who is now seventeen, meets me in the yard. He is dressed in camouflage with his shotgun. He is obviously going hunting. He calls out, "Daddy, do you think I've got enough daylight left to get down on the creek where the wood ducks usually are?"

I assure him he has plenty of time, even though today is one of the shortest days of the year. I think of how much I would enjoy going with him, but the loud cry of the manuscript calls out my name. Then, it seems as if these words come out of my mouth before I even realize it: "Clint, would it mess up your hunt if I went with you?"

He responds as to how I'd be very welcome to go with him. I hurriedly put on my camo and we load into the truck. We go to a spot on Bundick Creek where there are nearby sloughs, usually holding water and wood ducks, during the winter. The thought of shooting ducks is not a big deal to me. I'm just going to enjoy being in the woods with my son and our faithful dog, Ivory.

For the next two hours we creep through the woods, speaking very little. However, the conversation in my heart is steady and warm. To be outside on a beautiful Christmas eve is special in itself, but to have uninterrupted time with Clint is the best part of the afternoon.

We hunt hard and walk a good distance but find no ducks. The recent heavy rains have swollen the creek and pushed the ducks out of the sloughs where we usually find them. Nevertheless, the hunt is not a failure. When you are in the woods, it is always a successful time and positive investment, no matter what the results are.

We tromp back to the road weaving our way through the thick maze of briars and potholes of water. Ivory runs through the underbrush showing the simple joy of a hunting dog in the woods with her two masters. Now that our hunt is over and darkness approaches, we unload our guns and walk side by side as we visit.

Reaching the highway we look westward and see a beautiful red sunset through the nearby bare trees. Clint remarks that it may be the prettiest sunset he's ever seen and I readily agree. I believe our time spent together has a lot to do with why this sunset looks even brighter to me.

We reach the bridge and cross it to get back to our truck. As we walk across the bridge, I look down on Bundick Creek at our old swimming spot. The fast current and dark water flowing level with the bank doesn't look like a place you'd want to swim on this cold day. As I look at this special spot- the scene of so many wonderful afternoons spent as a boy growing up, and later with my own boys, I realize how long it has been since I wrote the "First Swim of the Summer" story you've just read.

Our days of creek swimming are basically over. We still swim but it is always at the camp pool, and many times the boys go without me. Clay and Clint still slip off to the creek occasionally but they are at the age where they'd never want to be seen swimming with their dad.

I stop for a brief moment looking southward. I'm sure Clint and Ivory think I'm checking downstream for one last sign of ducks. But, I'm just observing the fast flow of the creek. I wonder how long it will take the water flowing by us to reach the Ouiska Chitto, then the Calcasieu River, and finally the Gulf of Mexico at Cameron.

I'm also thinking about the last ten years and how they've flown so rapidly by just as the water in this creek. In a few more months, Clint will join his brother Clay away from home at college. Even though he'll come home often, his mom and I know it will not be the same as he begins life on his own. That is not a complaint, but a simple stating of the truth. I know this pattern of breaking away is as it should be, but the realization fills me with both wonder and sadness.

During the coming year there will only be three of us at the supper table. Terry will still eat his share, but there will be two less hungry teenagers with us at mealtime.

Looking one last time at the creek, I realize the next time I probably will be creek swimming is in five or ten years with my own grandchildren.

"Lord, help me gather every precious second and moment of all of these blessings You've sent my way. Teach me to number my days. Remind me of the importance of creek swims, duck hunts, and anything else that can be a memory-making and growing time with these boys you've given me."

Professor Cavanaugh's Best Lecture

Nervously I stood in the hallway outside the Louisiana College biology department's second floor office, waiting to see Professor Cavanaugh. I'd been standing here for several minutes, my chemistry book under one arm, and a class drop sheet in the other.

Professor Charles J. Cavanaugh was a Louisiana College institution. "Prof" as he was affectionately known, had taught biology there for over thirty years. He was the most beloved and respected teacher at Louisiana College. At first glance he seemed to be an unassuming and ordinary man. However on my first day of biology class, when he strode to the podium and began lecturing without any notes, it was obvious I was in the presence of greatness. This man was a master teacher, who blended a serious love of teaching with a kindly smile and a sharp sense of humor.

Prof. Cavanaugh taught both of my freshmen biology courses. Without a doubt, he was the most awe-inspiring teacher I'd ever encountered. Never once in those two semesters did I see him use any notes- everything came from his memory and years of experience. His unique method of teaching made the material seem to come alive. Students in his classes never came in late or talked during the lectures. To be in his lectures was to be in the presence of a master at work.

He was so admired and respected at Louisiana College that the school renamed the Science and Math Building as "Cavanaugh Hall," even while he was still an active teacher working there.

So, I had some what of a reason to be nervous as I stood outside the office door of this legend. The reason I was here was out of sheer desperation. The previous year, I had selected science education as my major- largely due to the powerful influence of Prof. Cavanaugh's biology teaching.

However, during my trek toward this goal of being a science teacher, I had run into a seemingly insurmountable obstacle- it was called Chemistry 105. Being from a rural school, my chemistry background was pretty weak. In fact after two weeks of class, they'd covered everything I knew, plus a heck of a lot I didn't. I desperately found myself drowning in a raging sea of formulas, equations, and complex problems. I was distraught, discouraged, and felt hopeless.

I really felt confused and lost. Realistically, I fully understood I probably could not pass this course- not just this semester, but most likely never. I saw my dream of teaching science going down the drain. With resignation, I went by the registrars' office and picked up a drop slip. My plan was to take the test tomorrow, and after I failed it, simply drop the chemistry class the next day.

After picking up the drop slip, I impulsively went to Cavanaugh Hall and decided to see Prof. Cavanaugh, before heading back to my dorm to lick my wounds.

So, there I stood peering in the window of his office, watching him walking back and forth, gathering papers. My courage melted and I turned to leave. I told myself he probably wouldn't even remember me from last year's classes. But before I could chicken out and leave, Professor Cavanaugh came walking out the door.

Impulsively, I blurted out, "Could I talk to you?" I'm sure my voice and face had the sound and look of desperation. Prof. Cavanaugh stopped with an armload of papers and smiled as he said, "Sure."

So, I began my tale of woe to this kindly old gentleman. I shared how I really felt it was God's will for me to become a science teacher. However, with my inability to grasp chemistry, I saw no course but to drop the class and leave behind my dream of science teaching.

Before I could continue, he interrupted me and spoke. His kindly smile tightened as he firmly said, "God's will?

God's will?" Son, I'll tell you what God's will is for you- Get in there, work, and pass chemistry. That's what God's will is for you!"

He didn't say it unkindly, but he said it with definite conviction. His face had turned slightly red as he passionately issued this challenge to me.

I really don't know if he said anything else, because I was in such shock. I'd come for encouragement from this great man and instead had received a brief, brisk, and clear lecture. Prof. Cavanaugh turned and strode down the hallway, leaving me in the wake of the words he'd just spoken. I felt about two inches tall and it was as if my own grandpa had just given me a stern lecture.

Well, I studied chemistry hard that night. I took the test the next day simply determined to do my best. Miraculously, I passed it! Well to be perfectly honest, I passed it with the lowest possible D, but much to my shock, I had really passed this test.

But the greatest miracle was what happened inside me. I decided that very day as to how nothing was going to stop me from achieving my goal of teaching. Prof's challenge in the hallway had lit the fire of determination in me. I was going to pass this course or die trying.

One day, a month or so later in chemistry lab, my teacher, Dr. Dennis Watson, called me to the side and as he eyed me suspiciously said, "What's happened to you?" I really believe he thought I'd either had a brain transplant or was a very crafty cheater.

The fact that I eventually made an A in both the lecture and lab was no great reflection on me, but rather a tribute to the fire Professor Cavanaugh's speech lit in me. His "lecture" in the hallway of the building bearing his name taught me this spiritual truth, which is so important to grasp: Most of the time God's will is much simpler than we choose to make it. It can usually be summed up this way- *Do your best where you are, and bloom where you are planted . . . and don't quit.*

It's been over twenty-five years since Prof. Cavanaugh taught me. I've probably forgotten most of the biology knowledge he instilled in me. I'm pretty rusty on mitosis, DNA models, and cell structure. However, his lecture in the hallway still reverberates in my heart. When I've found myself in tough times, as we all do throughout life, I've taken solace in the words of this wise old professor who reminded me of the importance of perseverance and hard work.

Yes, I did go on to teach both biology and chemistry. What a great time I had teaching young students about the wonders of science. Sometimes, during the year, in my senior chemistry classes, I would open my worn college chemistry book and take out a faded, yellowed dog-eared blank drop slip and share this story. Once again, I was reminded, even as I told them, that in life we all face times when it seems hopeless and we feel lost and confused. But that is always the exact time to buckle down, work hard, and find God's will, by simply doing our best.

Yes, God's will, most often, it is simply doing the best we can, right where we are placed.

O Christmas Tree!

My next-door neighbor, Mitzi Foreman, walks through our Christmas tree field. It is a cold and clear Sunday afternoon three weeks before Christmas. We search through the area where last week she tagged her tree. But it is to no avail- we cannot find the tree with her tag on it. This is embarrassing because Mitzi is my neighbor and friend, and now I can't find her tree. We talk as we continue looking and finally I tell her, "Well, maybe your tag blew off or it could be worse- maybe someone pulled it off." All of the other nearby good-sized trees are taken.

My dad and I have learned to be prepared for situations like this in our Christmas tree business. We have several extra trees tagged just for such an occurrence as this. When we need a special tree, such as in a situation like this, we've got a backup plan. I show Mitzi a beautiful tall Leyland cypress in the southeast corner of our field. Mitzi immediately loves it and instructs me to cut it. After I load it in her truck, she leaves a satisfied customer, and I am a very relieved salesman. Once again, I go back and look for her original tree, but no tag or large tree is visible anywhere.

Later that afternoon, my dad joins me and together we look for the missing Foreman tree. Then daddy spots it-- the rough-cut stump of a tree. Except this one has not been cut with the level clean cut of our bucksaw. It has a sharp angled cut probably done with a machete or brush hook. Now we know what happened to the Foreman tree- someone stole it.

This just mystifies me. Who in the world would steal a Christmas tree? That is pretty bad and low. I told Daddy that I just couldn't imagine a family sitting there on Christmas morning, opening presents, and singing "Silent Night" around a stolen Christmas tree.

However, sadly, people will steal just about anything. In our camp gift shop, we have a minor problem with shoplifting. Ironically, the most stolen item are the W.W.J. D. bracelets. As you probably know, this stands for "What Would Jesus Do?" Well, I know this much- Jesus wouldn't tell you to steal a bracelet– or for that matter, a Christmas tree.

What especially irks me about this stolen tree is how each year we give free trees to needy folks. All the "Grinch" who stole the tree would have needed to do was ask, and we'd been happy to help. Well, a fellow could drive himself crazy wondering about these kinds of things, or trying to figure out who the culprit was. I content myself with the fact as to how they must have needed the tree more than we did.

Then a few days later while in the front yard, I walk to our front door. Hanging from the Christmas wreath on the door is a scribbled note telling how someone had cut a tree during the day. Attached to the note, held there by a clothespin, is a twenty-dollar bill. Taking the note and money down, I kneel to look under our doormat. Sure enough, there is another one of our price tags, a ribbon, and another twenty dollars. Written on the price tag is a nice note wishing us a Merry Christmas.

Each year, daddy puts up a sign telling how we operate our tree business. I love his handwritten sign at the end of our road: "If we aren't home, you can still get your tree. The saw is on the front porch. You can leave your tag, your name, and money by the front door. Now go do your thing."

Believe it or not, this system has worked well over the years. We've found that when you put trust in people, they will usually come through in an honest way.

Once, we had several trees, out near the highway, stolen over the period of a week. We knew the thieves must be coming at night and slipping out to the trees which are between our house and the highway. It really bothered me and I told the boys that if they heard or saw any vehicles stopping on the road, to alert me.

One night just about 10:30 p.m., Clint and I saw the headlights of two vehicles leaving our driveway. We sprang into action and ran to the garage, backed out the truck, and took off in hot pursuit. We were really dressed for a fight– I had on my pajamas and Clint was in his boxers and a T-shirt. Driving fast to catch up with the fleeing vehicles, we knew we finally had the tree stealers caught red-handed!

We caught up with them at the intersection where Dry Creek's only two highways intersect. The moment of truth was upon us. Our truck headlights illuminated the rear of both vehicles. There the culprits were- my mom in her van and my dad in his truck.

It seemed they'd left the Christmas tree field after dark to go to a basketball game. So they could ride together, they'd left one vehicle out by the trees. Clint and I both burst out laughing at our misadventure. We turned the truck around without even stopping them. Arriving back home, DeDe was waiting at the door. We told her our story and she asked, "Well, what would you boys have done if you'd caught up with the real thieves?"

Sheepishly, we looked at each other in our nightclothes and I replied, "I guess I would have taken off my house shoe and whipped them with it."

We've had plenty of laughter with that story and we've also had fun with our tree farm. Through our tree business, many new friendships have begun. We've watched families of five come and look for hours, hunting the perfect tree. Then, I've seen men come at nine o'clock at night, park their truck at an angle so the headlights could illuminate the nearby rows, and hurriedly get out. You can tell they've been reluctantly sent by their wives to get a tree. They usually walk up to the first tree by the road and curtly say, "Cut that one." Kneeling down with my saw, I always say,

"Now, are you sure?" The reply is usually along the lines of, "Yeah, the old lady told me to get a tree and that one there will be plenty good." Then as quickly as he drove up, this careful shopper is gone.

Then, there is just something about the human condition that makes us think that bigger is better. Our niche in the Christmas tree market has always been five to seven foot high trees. We very seldom grow one more than seven foot high. However, even though most houses and mobile homes have an eight-foot ceiling, everyone wants a nine-foot tree. It really is something to observe, but I guess it is human nature, or at least American nature, to think the bigger, the better. As an example, just look at our fast food places, where you now can "super size" everything.

With our Christmas trees, we've really had fun with children. The excitement of warmly dressed preschoolers running through the trees laughing and singing is enough to put anyone in the Christmas spirit. The fun of letting a five-year-old boy hold the other end of the saw as he "helps" me cut down a tree. As the tree falls over he loudly shouts, "Timmmbbbbeeer." He'll remember for the rest of his life how he "cut down that tree" during a Christmas season so many years ago.

One of my favorite experiences, illustrating how special a tree is to a young child, occurred about five years ago. A preschool class from East Beauregard School came to shop for a tree for their classroom. Several of the parents came and helped their child also select a tree for home. It was fun walking with them as they ran from one large tree to another, accompanied by our barking dogs.

After choosing and cutting four or five trees, the preschoolers loaded back on the bus. I put the trees in the back of my truck and began following the bus to school. About half way down my driveway, the bus suddenly came to an abrupt stop. Teacher Dianne Brown exited the bus and came back to me. She hurriedly told me that one little boy had begun to cry and shout, "I want my tree. That man is taking my tree. I want my tree right now!" It took a few minutes of careful explanation to convince him we were bringing his tree to school.

Yes, stolen Christmas trees could make you cynical, but the joy in the faces of children and their families cutting a tree on a cold late afternoon causes the theft to fade from my mind. The family of four who just left with their tree will decorate it tonight after supper. Everyone will join in and help as the Christmas season comes alive in their home.

The occasional person who takes advantage of us is greatly outnumbered by the folks who are as honest as the day is long. Our honor system works well because of this: Most people are good down in their hearts. In life we must decide whether people are either rascals, or that they are basically honest. There are plenty of examples of each belief, to see and use, to support either view. The important thing is the attitude which we choose to take on our view of mankind.

I recall other signs of a basic trust in our community: A turnip green patch along the highway with a crude lettered sign inviting people to pick all of the greens they need and leave their money in the mailbox.

Another special long-time example of trust in our community is found at Farmer's Dairy. An empty butter dish serves as the bank for people who come throughout the day and night for a gallon of fresh thick milk. This honor system has been in use for years and Mr. Matt Farmer told me it has worked very well.

An old story relates how a wise man sat each day at the gate of his city. He would observe the coming and goings of the day. One day a young man, obviously a stranger, approached the city gate.

The traveler asked the old man, "What kind of town is this?" This wise old man, as men of wisdom often do, asked the traveler his own question: "Well, what kind of town did you come from?"

The young man began a long tirade against his former city. According to him, everyone was unkind, unfriendly, and took advantage of him.

After the young traveler ended his complaining, the wise man finally answered the original question, "Well son, this town is exactly like the one you came from."

The young traveler immediately turned and continued down the road looking for a "good town." Chances are he never found this good town, because he would not have recognized it even had he entered it.

Later the same day, a second traveler came to the city gates. He approached the wise man and asked the very same question as the first visitor, "Sir, what kind of town is this one?"

The wise man thoughtfully looked into the eyes of the young man and asked, "What kind of town did you come from?"

This second traveler began, "I come from a wonderful town. It's where I grew up and the people there are very nice and friendly."

Before the traveler could continue speaking, the old man interrupted him. He stated, "Well son, this town is exactly like your home town."

It is true- In life we find exactly what we are looking for. Our attitude and outlook determines how we perceive the world around us.

Back in my field, as I am standing beside the cut trunk of that stolen Christmas tree, I'm reminded of what Victor Frankl, who survived the Nazi concentration camps, said,

"Every freedom can be taken from a man. But there is one freedom which no one can take from you- the choice of your attitude."[2]

In life we can see every person as a potential Christmas tree thief, or we can see them as the person who'll honestly cut their own tree and leave the money under the doormat. It is a choice, and the choice is ours to make.

[1] *Man's Search For Meaning*
Victor Frankl copyright 1959

"Six Foot Deep" in Trouble

One of my ministries is to work with people in selecting their grave sites at Dry Creek Cemetery. I've found that this is a time when we can really help people. I call it the "open window of opportunity." Whether it's a kind word, a hand on the shoulder, or a whispered prayer, people are always open to help during their time of grief.

The openness of people to being helped is because the loss of a loved one, and the accompanying grief, brings forth such strong emotions. These emotions may vary from tears, regret, anger, and sometimes-even laughter. Because the emotions at this time are so raw and close to the surface, anything that creates extra stress can really affect people.

For many years my partner in grave marking was Mr. Jay Miller. He took me under his wing and taught me how to find the corners of a families' grave plot and reminded me of how families were kin to each other and where they should be buried. Last November, Mr. Jay was buried in the very cemetery he loved so greatly.

He had died in a way that touched everyone who knew and loved him. Early on the morning of his death, he went deer hunting with his daughter and pastor. After putting each of them on a stand, he was walking to his deer stand when he fell dead. I heard several men in Dry Creek say, "I can't think of a better way to go than how Mr. Jay did." He was healthy at eighty-three, with the ones he loved, and able to be still be doing what he enjoyed most.

I miss him, especially when it comes time to mark a grave. I depended on him for his experience and wisdom in handling touchy matters at the cemetery. However, most of all I miss his friendship. I still look for his red truck to pull up at the post office like clockwork each morning at precisely 8:30.

Mr. Jay's grandson, Mark, has taken his job as the grave marker. Mark is great and we'll enjoy working together on this, but we both know that so much knowledge of this cemetery left us last November.

Probably because of that, we've both been concerned to get each grave in the right spot. We have a deep fear of messing up. And if you mess up on the placing of a grave, real trouble and pain can result for the families involved. So, these anxious thoughts came to me last Thursday when I was called on to mark not one, but two graves. Both of these burials were to be on Saturday, with both being handled by the same funeral home, Labby Memorial of DeRidder.

The thought hit me that it was essential to get each grave marked clearly so there could be no confusion. In the back of my mind, I imagined what it would be like if they got confused and put one of the deceased in the wrong spot. It was not a pretty thought to entertain as I imagined the chaos and chagrin that would result from a mistake like this.

I used special care in marking each grave. After driving the markers down, I put flagging with the family names on each one. To be sure everything was right, I called Mrs. Labby and explained to her exactly where each grave was located. She said Roy, their usual gravedigger, was off work on Saturday. She informed me that Roy's helper, Willie, would be coming.

It's a country tradition that normally they don't "open a grave" (that's what they call the process of digging a grave) until the morning of the funeral. This is to avoid problems in the event of rain. I think it's also to avoid all of those stories about people falling in open graves.

A fictional story has always been told of a village which had a shortcut path through the local cemetery. One evening, just at dusk, an elderly farmer was walking this path just as night fell. In the gathering darkness, he got off the path and fell right into a freshly dug grave. After much effort, he realized he couldn't get out of the six-foot deep hole. Finally he gave up, sat down, and waited for daylight and rescue.

Eventually a second man, the town drunk, staggered along this same cemetery path and he fell into the same grave. In the darkness on this moonless night, the drunk struggled with all of his might to get a toehold and climb out. Finally, exhausted, he also sat down to wait for help the next morning. It was at this precise moment the old farmer put his hand on the drunk's shoulder in comfort and said, "There's no use trying, neither one of us can get out of here."

Yet, the farmer was wrong, because the drunken man, fueled by both fear and adrenaline, climbed right out of the grave and ran for his life as he stumbled over headstones and markers. I smile slightly as I remember this story. It is one more good reason not to dig these two graves until Saturday, the day of the funeral.

On Friday, the day before the two funerals, I go to the cemetery just to check the markers. Everything is just exactly as I've marked it. Just to be sure, I call the funeral home one more time and double check ensuring that we are all on the same page.

It is at this point I make my biggest mistake- I relax and tell myself that it's all straight and taken care of. With all of my calls and clear markings at the cemetery, there is no way they can get it confused. Therefore, I don't feel I need to be present for the grave digging the next morning.

That Saturday dawns as one of the prettiest days of the year. March always has some of the best weather in Louisiana. The dogwoods and azaleas are in full bloom. On this day, the sky is a perfect blue and a cool pleasant wind blows.

At the camp where I work, we are hosting a Deacons Conference. It's an event I've really been excited about having. After breakfast I join the men for the morning's first session. It is a wonderful time as these men share and pray together.

It's about mid-morning when Linda Farmer, one of our cooks, calls me out of the meeting. I think to myself, "Now what in the world could be so important right now?" Linda's words shock me and send a literal chill down my spine: "They're on the phone from the funeral home. They think their man has dug the grave in the wrong spot."

My son Clint has my truck today, so I'm on foot. I quickly borrow Linda's van, grab my cemetery map from the office, and rush the two miles to the cemetery. As I glance at my watch it is already 10:45. The first funeral, at a church about thirty miles away, starts in fifteen minutes.

As I approach the cemetery, the first thing I see is the bright orange grave marker and the opened grave, and instantly I can see it's been dug in the wrong spot. The grave has been dug one row to the south from the spot I originally marked it. There, right next to the grave of my Papa's best friend, Luther Spears, is a yawning six-foot deep by seven-foot long grave. It's dug right in the spot where my beloved first grade teacher, Mrs. Ora Spears, will one day be laid to rest next to her husband.

On the other side of the grave is a three-foot high pile of sticky red clay. I'm thinking to myself that we've got a lot of work to do to get out of this mess.

The gravedigger, Willie, an older black man, is standing right beside the grave. He is nervously jumping from foot to foot as if he is standing on hot coals. Next to Willie is a younger man who is leaning on a shovel. Willie, sweating profusely, begins explaining how the marker was placed right against the Spears headstone. To prove my point, I show him where I had originally placed the marker.

Over and over he repeats himself, "I just dug it right where the marker was!" I answer back with, "Well, it's sure not where I marked it!" Quickly I realize that we've got to stop arguing, think fast, and work together. Looking at my watch, I'm shocked to see it is now after 11:00. The first funeral has started. Mentally I try to estimate the time needed for the service, family time, and thirty-mile trip to the cemetery.

I put my hand on Willie's shoulder and say, "Look, it's neither one of our faults this grave is in the wrong spot, but we've got to work together to get it in the right spot. You need to start digging the grave in the right spot. We'll fill in the other hole. Do you think we can get it ready?"

Willie shakes his head doubtfully. "I'm not sure there's enough time. And then I've still got to dig that second grave."

I try to comfort Willie by saying, "Look, I read in the obituaries where the 11:00 funeral was going to be led by four preachers. I've been around preachers enough to know it'll be a while before they get here. We've got plenty of time to straighten out this mess if we work together. Then, the second funeral is not until 3:00 anyway. We've got time."

I think to myself, "I'm sure going to be here when you start on that second grave over in the northwest corner."

Then I say to Willie, "Let's pray about this." There right by the open grave we pray. Willie holds his hat in his hands and passionately "amens" every sentence of my intercessory prayer for these two families and our task in front of us. Then we go to work.

Willie gets back on the backhoe and pushes some of the red clay back into the open hole and quickly moves to begin the new gravesite. I get the other worker to help me and we begin filling in the first grave with our shovels. Over in the other corner of the cemetery two of the caretaker's sons are weed eating around graves. I call for them to come help us. Gladly, these two strapping Mennonite boys come over, grab a shovel and go to work with us.

I can't help but occasionally look up to check on Willie. He really is an artist with the backhoe. He expertly maneuvers the scoop up and down until a deep rectangular grave begins to emerge.

Willie is still sweating heavily, and it's not really a warm day. Every once in a while, above the noise of the backhoe, I hear Willie saying, "Help me Jesus. Lord, help me Jesus."

From time to time he nervously takes a sideways glance toward the entrance road. I know he is fully expecting a big black hearse and a line of cars to come around the curve at any moment.

The other worker keeps the sides of the grave straight. He puts his shovel handle into the grave to mark its correct depth. Soon the grave is finished. We all help move the funeral home tent, and they begin setting up the equipment and boards for the coffin to lay on.

Willie moves his backhoe across the cemetery to the 3:00 gravesite. I stand under the tent and sincerely thank God as to how this mess got straightened out before either family arrived. My head hurts just thinking of the chaos there would have been if they had arrived and found a grave in the wrong spot.

Right there I came up with a plan. From now on, in addition to the marker, I will use a can of spray paint to outline a grave on the exact spot where the grave is to go. In addition, I'll write the name of the family inside the rectangle so no miscommunication can take place.

Seeing that Willie is now happily digging the second, or if you want to be exact, third grave of the day at Dry Creek Cemetery, I'm satisfied that this day of calamity is going to turn out all right in the end. Finally, after watching Willie long enough to feel comfortable, I leave.

I drive back to work in my "stolen" van. Back at the camp I don't think they even noticed I was gone. I'd like to slip back into the deacon's meeting, but I have to go to the kitchen to tell Linda and the other cooks this story. Some things, especially those embarrassing to you, need to be shared so everyone can enjoy it. It's so important for us to laugh at ourselves, because everyone else is already laughing at us anyway.

That afternoon, the funeral procession from the 11:00 service doesn't get to the cemetery until 3:00 PM. Someone told me it was a wonderful service celebrating a rich life lived for God. Instead of four preachers speaking, there were eleven speakers!

The second burial took place at about four o'clock without a hitch. Neither family even knew about our close call with calamity, and that is all right with me.

The next day, Sunday, I woke up with my head hurting. I'm not talking about a headache. I'm talking about the pain of what I quickly realized was sunburn. Right on the top of my head, where I once had hair, was badly sunburned. I asked myself, "Now, how did my head get sunburned?" Then I realized that yesterday in my dash to the cemetery, I had left my trusty baseball cap behind. Even though I was not in the sun more than two hours, it was enough for a hairless scalp to burn pretty bad.

As I dressed for church, I looked in the mirror at the sunburned top of my head. I thought to myself, "I'll never hear the end of it about my sunburn when I get to church." The thought of Sharon Swisher, one of our deacon's wives, made me cringe. Every Sunday morning she greets every one of the bald men in our church with a lipstick-smeared kiss on the peak of their head. On this particular Sunday, I don't want anyone touching or kissing my painful crown.

Going out the door, I looked in the hallway mirror for one last inspection. I realized that my head and face was really pretty red. However, they weren't nearly as red as if we'd buried someone in the wrong grave...on that beautiful spring day at Dry Creek Cemetery when we were... "Six foot deep" in trouble.

The Friendship Lane

The most important trip you may take in life is meeting people halfway.
- Henry Boye

My favorite movie is the Christmas classic, "It's A Wonderful Life." I've seen it dozen of times and still cry at the end when George Bailey, played by Jimmy Stewart, is surrounded by his many friends and family who've come to rescue him from financial ruin and scandal.

As this large crowd sings "Hark the Herald Angels Sing," George Bailey holds a book. Inside the cover of the book, "The Adventures of Tom Sawyer," is an inscription from his guardian angel, Clarence Oddbody. It simply says, "Remember, no man is a failure who has friends."

One of God's greatest blessings are friends- People on whom you can depend in any situation. Friends who have stood steadfastly with you through both thick and thin times. My mom always told me, "Curt, always remember, you can't have too many friends." And as usual, my mom was right. Each and every friendship we have is a priceless jewel in our journey of life.

Great friendships take work and time. They don't just happen by accident. A deep and lasting friendship is built on shared experiences and love. Deep friendships are built on selfless giving on the part of both people. I've noticed that special friends seem to try to "out give" each other in kindness and help. A true friendship will always involve give and take.

If you ever visit Dry Creek, there is a special spot I'd like to show you. It is an overgrown pathway in the woods that bears witness to the importance of friendship between neighbors. Most people will walk right by this narrow passageway and never notice it, but it always catches my attention because of what it means.

This special place is what I call "The Friendship Lane." It is located just east of camp property, near the home of Frank Bogard. It is a ten-foot wide strip between two barbed wire fences. This path separates the land between the pioneer homesteads of Sereno Hanchey and Lionel Green. These two men, now dead for many years, were descendants of some of the earliest settlers of Dry Creek.

Mr. Rufus Hanchey, Sereno Hanchey's son, took me to "The Friendship Lane" just before he died. As we stood there, he related the following story:

"Curt, at some point many years ago, there was a difference of opinion between the Hanchey and Green families over where the property line, running east and west, was between our properties. Each family claimed to own land that reached over into the other's present field. Because there was no fence to stand as the dividing line, the actual land line was open to dispute."

Mr. Rufus continued, "My dad and Lionel Green had always been good friends, and they valued their friendship more than any piece of land and showed it by their actions. They met pretty close to where we are now standing and came up with a solution to this problem. They decided to declare the disputed ten-foot wide strip a "neutral zone." Each man would build a fence on their respective side of the strip. Together, they agreed to use the strip as a pathway, but neither would claim ownership. Due to this agreement, both families were satisfied and no further problem ever occurred."

As the son of a land surveyor, I've seen some pretty nasty fights between landowners over the difference of a two-foot strip along a fence. Some of the saddest things I've ever seen have been the sight of brothers and sisters falling out with each other over inherited land. I've seen family members go to their graves still holding a grudge against a brother or sister. How sad it is when we will let anything, material or temporary, break a priceless relationship with our families or neighbors.

Now I'm proud of the little plot of land I own. There is something special about walking your field and knowing the mud on your boots is yours. However, when I get to feeling as if this land really belongs to me, I get out my land abstract.

An abstract is a legal booklet showing the history of ownership of the land you now own. Thumbing through my abstract, I recognize some of the old family names that once lived in this area. It strikes me that some of these once well-known family surnames are no longer found in our area. They are now only names from the distant past.

Looking at my abstract, I also notice names of prior owners I've never heard of: Someone who owned this land for only a few months or several years. At this point, the sobering thought comes to me: One day this land I live on will belong to someone who will look at their updated abstract and wonder who the Iles family was that lived here at the beginning of the century.

I'm reminded that this land really doesn't belong to me. God, who is infinite, is just loaning it to me for a short finite period of time we call life. This thought helps me realize that there are many, many more things more important than being the biggest landowner around.

Standing at this overgrown path I call The Friendship Lane, I'm appreciative of these two men who placed friendship above an easily forgotten piece of land in the woods. People, and the relationships we develop through friendship, are much more important than any land title we can store in a bank safety deposit box or possession we can claim.

This "Friendship Lane" teaches me another lesson-- If we are going to get along with others, we need to give them a little room. Young people today call it "cutting some slack." If we push against, and rub on others, friction will result. And friction always generates heat, and heat can generate the fire of anger that, in time, harm and can ruin longtime friendships.

By simply giving others some space and walking away instead of fighting, the "friendship fences" in our lives can stay mended and in good shape. If we always have to "win" by getting our way, we will leave behind a trail of broken relationships, many of them with those closest to us. I'm often reminded of the saying, "You only have so much blood to spill, so choose your battles carefully."

Darkness is now approaching as I turn and leave the Friendship Lane. Glancing back one last time, I can visualize in my mind the long ago scene of Sereno Hanchey and Lionel Green walking their respective fields at sunset. They come upon each other and stop to visit. Each leans against his own fence, separated by the ten feet of land they share.

First one, then the other, crawls through his respective fence. They meet in this grassy neutral area where they shake hands and share a plug of chewing tobacco. As the sun sets behind the pines, they visit until it is so dark you can barely see them standing there. Only from the sound of their voices as they visit and laugh, can you tell they are standing back there, somewhere in the middle of the Friendship Lane.

The richest man in the world is not the one who still has the first dollar he has ever earned. It is the man who still has his best friends.
- Martha Mason

The Sweet Smell of Honeysuckle

Life is not improved by increasing its speed.
Gandhi

When spring arrives and everything is blooming, I always make time to go into Dry Creek swamp to check on the honeysuckle. Because I've spent all of my life in the Deep South, I don't know if wild honeysuckle bushes are found all over America. I simply know that when they bloom in early March there is nothing prettier or sweeter to smell.

The honeysuckle, or wild azalea as it is often called, is actually a small tree that more resembles a bush. It is found naturally along small streams and creeks, and doesn't grow very large. Other than a few weeks in the spring, it is unnoticed and unremarkable. However, when it blooms, it outshines every other tree or shrub in the swamp.

Another thing that makes it so special is its rarity. You won't find it growing along roadsides. Normally, you have to get off the beaten path to find honeysuckle. The fragrance of its pale pink blossoms is hard to describe. The "honey" in honeysuckle is the best way I know to describe its smell. It has a sweet smell that is pleasant to the nose and once you've enjoyed it, you never forget it. I've been in the woods after a spring rain and smelled honeysuckle long before I was near enough to see the bushes.

Because I'm on a honeysuckle kick and thinking about enjoying the little things in life, I even have my co-worker, Debra Tyler, who loves the outdoors as much as I do, put on the sign at the camp entrance, "Don't forget to stop and smell the honeysuckle."

During honeysuckle season, I always love to bring my wife, DeDe, a bouquet of honeysuckle. She places them in a vase which she then sets on the kitchen table. For several days, the fragrance greets you the instant you enter the house. That pungent, indescribable smell always makes me smile inside. It reminds me of childhood Sunday afternoon walks in the woods with my family. It was a time of less rushing about when people took more time to be together, often in the outdoors.

Honeysuckle time is when I always think of Mrs. Eleanor Andrews. No one in Dry Creek loves flowers, gardens, and plants more than Mrs. Andrews. Even though she has been an invalid for many years, she still has the prettiest yard in our community. She loves to sit by her window and point out the tulips, periwinkles, dogwoods, azaleas, and countless flowers as they each bloom in their respective seasons. Mrs. Andrews, my beloved fifth grade teacher, taught practically every young person in Dry Creek for over two decades. This sweet lady loves honeysuckle, and nature, as much as anyone I know.

Each year her son Charlie, who had a doctorate in horticulture, would bring her a beautiful bouquet of honeysuckle blossoms from the woods. She'd proudly display it on her kitchen table. When Charlie died suddenly a few years ago, spring came and the time for her honeysuckle bouquet arrived.

Loretta Bushnell Langley, who takes special care of Mrs. Andrews, told her dad about Charlie's bouquet. Sure enough the next week, Mrs. Andrews had her annual bouquet-- picked and prepared by Jessie Bushnell. I can just see Jessie driving up in his old truck with a bedful of barking dogs riding in the back. Dressed in his welder's cap and old overalls, he joyfully brings this gift to this special lady. I know how Jessie feels- just as if he is in elementary school again, bringing an apple to his favorite teacher.

Now, my annual job is to bring Mrs. Andrews a Christmas tree. I still break out in a cold sweat hoping the tree I selected meets her exacting eye. Once again I'm ten years old, handing in my multiplication tables to Eleanor Andrews.

I'm sure Jesse thinks the same thing as me when he approaches her porch, "Will I have this privilege next year, or will she be gone?" She is over eighty and not in good health. She has been my special friend for nearly forty years, and I can't imagine spring in Dry Creek without her presence.

Last week, Mrs. Andrews fell and hit her head. She was sent to the nearby Kinder hospital where they discovered she had double pneumonia. Then, she had a heart attack and was rushed to a larger hospital in Lake Charles. Since then she has steadily gone down. Loretta called me on the phone today, and we both cried as we tried to fathom what life would be like without this matriarch of our community.

All today, I've thought about so many special times I've had with her. I recall a recent January when the college football championship was held between Florida St. and Virginia Tech. I promised Mrs. Andrews, a true sports fanatic, the boys and I would come watch the game with her. When I drove up late from a meeting, there were five cars in her driveway. Knocking at the door, I saw boys everywhere. There was lot of noise and chanting back and forth. Seminole fans made the tomahawk chop while the boys for the Hokies cheered for Michael Vick to pull out victory for Virginia Tech.

...And in the midst of all this commotion, sat Mrs. Eleanor Andrews happily puffing away on a cigarette. I'll never forget the look of pure joy on her face. Her eyes seemed to glow from the enjoyment of being surrounded by young people having a good time. We had such a swell time watching the game together- all eleven of us. You can probably guess who enjoyed it the most- Eleanor Andrews.

Looking around on this special January night, I swear I could nearly smell the fragrance of honeysuckle in her living room, even in the midst of this cold winter night. Maybe it wasn't honeysuckle, but instead the equally sweet smell of love and friendship that could be felt tonight in this room.

When the game ended each boy came by her chair, leaned down, and gave her a hug. She kissed each one on the cheek as they bent down close to her. The sight of these big old country boys hugging on her touched me. She had lost two of her three sons to death, but for one precious night her house was once again full of laughing boys.

I waited at the end of the hugging line. As I leaned down, she grabbed my arm with a surprisingly strong grip, and pulled my head down and whispered in my ear, "You'll never know how much this meant to me." But I knew that without her saying . . . and it'd meant just as much to me to see my own boys picking and laughing with her as they sat together watching the game.

. . . But now, it is early March and she lays in the hospital fighting for her life . . . It's early spring and the plants are blooming here in Dry Creek. It's hard to believe Eleanor Andrews will probably die in the middle of her favorite time of year. I'd always thought she would leave us in the dead of winter, when the trees were bare and her garden was empty.

Late that night I returned from a meeting. As I neared home, it was after ten o'clock, but I stopped at the bridge over Mill Bayou anyway. In a light rain, I climbed the barbed wire fence and stepped carefully in the darkness toward the creek. I had my flashlight to watch for snakes. With its light, I found what I was looking for- a small honeysuckle bush. Due to a slight frost several nights ago and tonight's rain, most of the blossoms were gone. The remaining flowers were slightly wilted and drooping.

Carefully, so as not to further damage the blooms, I picked a bouquet of honeysuckle. The smell, so sweet and fragrant in the heavy night air, reminded me of how much I love spring.

As I'm re-climbing the fence, a truck pulled up behind my truck, which was parked on the shoulder of the highway. It was just Whitney Green, one of our local volunteer firefighters, checking to make sure there wasn't someone in need of help. I flashed my light at him and told him I was O.K. I bet he wondered what I was doing climbing this fence on a rainy night.

Whitney stopping to check on me during this dark rainy night reminds me of what I love about country life. There is a wonderful mixture of nosiness combined with concern that makes people butt into your business. They are not interfering to bother you, but rather to help as needed. Oh, the joys of country living!

Arriving home from my honeysuckle expedition, I carefully placed my bouquet in a green vase with water. The next morning, bouquet in hand, I leave early for the drive to St. Patrick's hospital in Lake Charles. Quietly, I ease in to the ICU where Mrs. Eleanor Andrews lay. Tubes and monitors are all around her, and her face is covered with an oxygen mask. When she sees me, I'm greeted with the smile that has lit up my life since I was eleven years old. I lean down close because her voice is very weak. In spite of the effort required to speak, she begins talking non-stop, the smile never leaving her face.

Most of what she says I cannot understand because of the oxygen mask. However, she says one sentence that I hear very clearly. She looks me squarely in the eyes and says weakly, "I'm going home today."

For a moment I think she's confused and believes she is going to her home in Dry Creek. When she reads the confusion on my face, she repeats in a stronger voice and with more emphasis on the word "home,"

"No, I'm going **home** today."

The look in her eyes and the smile on her face tell me even more than her words. She is going *home* and she's looking forward to it. She has suffered enough, most of her loved ones are already on the other side, and she's ready to go. Nothing, not even her beloved flowers and yard in Dry Creek, can cause her to want to stay on this earth any longer.

I lean down and kiss her on the cheek one last time. Walking out of the cubicle, I look back for one final glance. There, on the stand by her bed, is the green vase of honeysuckle. One last time I look back at her face, still smiling in spite of the oxygen mask covering her face. Once more, I glance at the honeysuckle bouquet, then wave goodbye, and walk away.

Mrs. Eleanor Andrews was wrong by one day. She died the next day at 10:30 a.m. on Thursday, March 16, 2000. When they called me with this news, my heart was filled with a selfish sadness, but there was no sadness for her because the suffering of her worn out body had ended. She knew the Lord personally, and as it is promised in scripture,

"Absent from the body . . . present with the Lord."[3]

She was now at home with her God.

My sadness is how we'll all miss her in Dry Creek. She was like a grandmother to me, and no one can replace your grandmother. I feel the most sorrow for our cooks at the camp. Mrs. Andrews was a special friend and ministry to our cooks at Dry Creek Camp. Betty, Linda, Shirley, Sheila, and Rea took her a plate of food every time they

[3] II Corinthians 5:8 (KJV)

cooked a meal. Because of their daily association with this sweet lady, they've lost a friend who will leave a void in their lives.

I firmly believe the meals brought by these ladies, and the love and kindness shown by her church family and friends like Loretta Langley and Paul Hanchey, all combined to allow her to live at home alone until the very end. There was a "beautiful conspiracy" to take care of her so she could continue independently living at home. All of us who love her always had the fear she would be forced to leave her yard and flowers, to reside in a nursing home.

In the days following her death, I think back to so many special memories of Eleanor Andrews. I smile as I remember how she favored boys in her class over the girls. Because I was a "Dry Creek boy," she gave me a little extra attention and did what the best teachers always do- she made me feel as if I was the most special student in the world.

Then I jump ahead thirty years to her seventy-eighth birthday. We held a party for her at the Old Dry Creek School building where she'd taught for so many years. She fussed at us for planning this event without her permission.

The actual week of the party, she was nervous and agitated. She kept saying, "No one is going to come. There won't be a hand full of people to see an old woman like me."

Sunday arrived and she was taken to the schoolhouse where she'd attended school and later taught. I avoided her because I wasn't sure if I was in her good graces due to this event. Then people began coming, and kept coming- a long receiving line of her grandchildren, country men who'd sat in her classroom, ladies who'd first been taught by her in Bible school, and old friends with whom she'd graduated from high school with in this very same building. What a special day it was for Eleanor Andrews!

When the party was over and the crowd cleared out, she gave me a look that froze me in my tracks. In that gravelly crackled voice I loved so much, she said, "Well, I guess I can forgive you now for planning this without my permission." Then she broke out into a huge smile and said, "Today, I've had one of the finest days of my entire life."

Then, once again, I return to that January Football night. I see her broad smile as Florida State scores and half of the boys go crazy while the other half make derisive comments. There is a picture that I will always have in my mind of this lovely lady surrounded by love, joy, and fun.

Pondering her death, I think about where is now. She'd been widowed from her precious husband, Red, for forty-one years. She'd buried two of her sons, Keith and Charlie. In my mind and heart, I can see the wonderful tearless reunion as she is greeted by loved ones, her parents, and former students and friends. It is a time of fellowship and smiles that is far better than any football game or birthday party. Best of all, this is a group that won't be separated ever again.

Driving home after her funeral on that sunny March day, I see that the honeysuckle at Mill Bayou has lost its last blossoms of the year. But deep down in my soul, I believe I can still smell the sweet and wonderful fragrance of honeysuckle.

A Homeless Lady

One of the things I love about Dry Creek Camp is the friendliness of folks who visit and work here. There is a special atmosphere of caring that I believe can only come from God.

On a recent weekend in January, our "ministry of hospitality" was tested in a unique way. Dwayne Quebedeaux, our projects director, is a caring and compassionate man. He and his wife, Allison, are always looking for ways to help folks. This helpful attitude is why he was touched as he neared the Tabernacle that day. What he saw was what appeared to be a homeless lady digging in the trash can. She was dressed in the way you've seen on the streets of big cities- several layers of old clothes, evidently all she owned, and shaggy hair sticking out from under a dirty scarf. She was pushing an old bicycle as she explored the area around the Tabernacle. Inside, a group of over one hundred ladies sang away, while outside, this poor woman dug in the trash.

Dwayne said his heart just went out to her. He'd just come out of the Dining Hall, home of those famous Dry Creek rolls. He approached the woman to invite her to come eat. She quickly turned her back and rapidly pushed the bike away.

Word had spread among our staff to this woman's plight and they began trying to get her to stop so they could help her. When she continued to walk away and hide, Dwayne did the only thing he knew to do- he called the Sheriff's Department to come help. Soon a deputy arrived, but there was no lady to be found.

Just as the deputy drove out the front gate, Dwayne saw the lady emerge from her hiding place. He was determined to help her so he once again approached her. This time she stopped as Dwayne came near. In a muffled voice she told him, "I'm with the Ladies Group. We're testing them to see if they will stop and help me."

Needless to say, Dwayne was floored. After hearing the story, all of our staff had a good laugh. However, we also told Dwayne he had "passed the test." He had stopped to help a person in need just as Jesus did. May the same be said of all of us.

And Jesus said, when you have done it unto the least of these my brethren, you have done it unto me. - Matthew 25:40

Brad's Hat

Bradley Robinson

As I load my gear up for a trip to Glorieta, New Mexico, I grab one last item- a weather-beaten and stained New York Yankees cap. Putting it on I'm reminded of the fact that I've never cared much for the Yankees. However, I'm not wearing this cap to be stylish or cool. Because this cap doesn't look too good anyway. But it's a special hat and that's why I'm wearing it to Glorieta, New Mexico, our National Southern Baptist Camp.

You see this hat was Brad's hat. If you read my first book, you will recall the stories of our beloved staffer, Brad Robinson. Brad was killed during the summer of 1999 when struck by a senseless drunken driver. After his death, I asked Bubba and Karan, his parents for only one possession of Brad's- his beloved Yankees cap. The first time I met Brad in the spring of 1998 he was wearing this cap. And the last time I ever saw him, as he made popcorn at camp on the day before he was killed, he wore that faded and stained dark blue cap.

It really looked ragged after two summers of mowing, life guarding, and cleaning plates in the "pigpen." Once I asked Brad if he liked the Yankees. He replied with a smile, "No, but I've always liked their hat." Therefore, even though I don't care for the Yankees either, I am wearing Brad's hat as we head west to New Mexico.

Eight members of staff are traveling as a group in the camp van. We spend the first day of our trip traversing across Texas. I recall the ditty that goes this way,

"The sun has risen
The sun has set,
And here I am in Texas yet."

Entering Texas heading west on Interstate 10 at Orange, there is a sign that always catches my attention. It reads: El Paso 892 miles. Texas is a big state and you can drive a long ways just looking at mesquite trees and farmland. After a full day of driving, the camp van reaches our stop for the first night at Big Country Baptist Camp near Abilene, Texas. This part of Texas is completely flat. You can see forever across the plains. Big Country Camp is on the banks of one of the forks of the Brazos River. At supper that evening is when I first meet Seth Martin. He is the son of the camp's maintenance director. He becomes my official guide to touring Big Country Camp.

I immediately notice a special maturity about Seth. Even though he is only fourteen, he seems to be much older and has a readily observable spiritual depth to him. Maybe it's just because Brad has been on my mind, or maybe it's the Yankees cap I have on, but Seth reminds me of Brad Robinson. Physically, they don't resemble each other, but there is a spiritual resemblance and maturity that touches my heart. Seth has that same way about him that quietly but confidently says, "God and I are going places together. Do you want to come along?"

Seth leads me down by the Brazos River, and as we walk he shares his interests and dreams. He is very easy to talk to and seems very comfortable telling about his life. Once again, I think of Brad and the wonderful talks we had together.

When I leave the next morning, I invite Seth to come visit us at Dry Creek the next summer and work a few weeks as a staffer. I'm once again reminded that one of the most important ministries we have at Dry Creek is growing, teaching, and mentoring young men and women.

Two days later we arrive at Glorieta. It is a large and beautiful camp nestled in the mountains near Santa Fe, New Mexico. Our staff, joined by hundreds of other camp leaders, has a wonderful four days of fellowship, worship, learning, and fun. As I walk the vast grounds of this famous camp, once again I think of Brad. ...Of how if he had lived, he would one day have come here. I could see him bringing young people here. Brad, though only seventeen, was the unquestioned leader of his own church youth group and always planning things for them.

One of his goals was to be a youth leader. He would have been a great one with the leadership skills he possessed and his love for God. In my mind I could see Brad, at an older age, coming to speak at Glorieta to a large youth conference. He was a gifted communicator and loved preaching. In September 1998, while at the camp, he had surrendered to the ministry. In the months prior to his death, he was beginning to have many opportunities to preach in churches. I could easily see "Dr. Brad Robinson" holding a full chapel at Glorieta spellbound, or better yet- a full Tabernacle of youth at Dry Creek Camp.

Then I laugh as I recall another of Brad's goals. He would come up to me and say, "Bro. Curt, I hate to tell you, but I'm going to take your job from you someday. You'd better find something else to be looking at." We'd laugh together, but I knew he probably meant it. Looking around at Glorieta, I think to myself, "Brad probably would've thought he could run this place too, and he probably would've have been right."

Once again I smile as I recall a recent visit from Karan, Brad's mom. Karan showed me a letter she had recently received addressed to Brad from the President of the United States, Bill Clinton. This letter arrived several months after Brad's death. From reading the president's response in the letter, evidently Brad had written him sometime earlier in 1999, giving the President some timely advice on how to better run our country. President Clinton's reply was kind and thanked Brad for his input.

Karan and I both laughed as we wondered what subject Brad had decided to correct the President on. Brad Robinson had an opinion on everything and was not shy to share it, evidently even with the President of the United States.

Before leaving our conference at Glorieta, I had a sweet time of worship with the Lord. As I sat in the chapel, I really felt God's presence and peace. Verses just flooded into my heart:

The words of Jesus in John 14: "I am going there to prepare a place for you..."

-"Eye has not seen, nor ear heard, the things God has prepared for those who love him..."

And in my heart of hearts, I could see Brad's smile again. The smile that I'll always love, and I heard his voice saying, "It is so good here... I wouldn't want to come back, not to Glorieta, not to my precious family in Hicks, or even to the place I loved like heaven- Dry Creek Camp. Being in the presence of Jesus is so much better."

Then I recall a fable from my childhood:

Dragonfly larvae live in the water. As they mature, they develop their wings and then the ability to breathe. According to this fable, as a mature larva prepares to rise to the surface and fly away, the water-bound larvae make it promise to come back and tell what life is like up there above the water. Each emerging dragonfly faithfully promises to return soon and tell all about life flying in the air.

. . . However, no dragonfly ever returns to share. And the reason is simple: Because it is so wonderful freely flying around, they never get around to reporting back.

With this story swirling in my heart, I get up from the Glorieta chapel and leave. Coming outside into the cold February mountain air, I put Brad's hat back on and stand for a long time, just staring up into the bright blue sky...

The Tennessee Waltz . . . on a Linoleum Rug

Earlier this year, while reading the newspaper, a small article tucked into an inside page caught my attention. It was only a few lines and was easy to miss. The byline was from Louisville, Kentucky and told of the death of "PeeWee" King. To most people the name probably meant nothing, but when I saw his name one thing instantly came to my mind- "The Tennessee Waltz."

PeeWee King and fellow band member, Red Stewart wrote "The Tennessee Waltz" as they rode one day in Stewart's truck. According to them, the words were written on the back of an unfolded matchbox. The song quickly became a classic and has been recorded by hundreds of musicians of every musical style.

It has always been one of my favorite songs and here is why....

My family has always loved music. When the Old House was built at the end of the 19th century, music was an integral part of the family in the original one room. The fiddle was the family instrument of choice. My great-grandmother, Dosia, was first given a gourd fiddle made by her dad. Later she got a real one and began a love affair with fiddle music for the rest of her life.

As I write this story, I'm sitting in the original log room of the Old House. In front of me stands an old pump organ which has sat against the wall since 1903. It was bought by my great-great grandparents so their other daughter, Louise, could accompany her fiddle-playing sister. As I look at the old organ, now silent and in disrepair, I wonder at the sacrifice this family made to purchase this instrument. It is told in my family that Grandpa Wagnon saved money from several years of timber sales to buy the organ.

My grandfather, Lloyd Iles, inherited the love of fiddle music from his mother. Family gatherings at the Old House were always accompanied by music. My Aunt Margie on the piano, was joined by my dad singing and chording on his guitar, as my grandfather and great grandmother played their fiddles. Of all the songs they played, the song I remembered best was The Tennessee Waltz. My dad and grandfather in their rich bass voices would tell this painful story of lost love:

I was dancing with my darling to the Tennessee Waltz,
When an old friend I happened to see.
I introduced him to my loved one,
And while they were dancing
My friend stole my sweetheart from me.

As Papa sang it, I would lay on the cold linoleum floor near his amplifier. Long before electric fiddles were sold, he had rigged up a way to give his fiddle an electric sound. I'd get as close as I could stand with my ear right next to the amp. As he played the mournful fiddle instrumental, I could just picture a young cowboy watching helplessly as his best friend swept away his girl as they danced together. Even as a young boy, who at that time hated girls, I was struck equally by both the sadness and beauty of this song.

The rich loud sound of the fiddle flowed through the room. Other family members sat in the room in straight chairs, careful to balance themselves on the uneven floor, which had been unlevel since the winds of Hurricane Audrey shifted this log house on its foundation in 1957.

I laid there and looked up at the original peeled pine logs in the ceiling. Directly behind my Grandpa was a large framed picture of him as a four-year-old child. He was dressed in a type of little frilled dress. This was the normal way small children were tortured in the early part of the Twentieth Century. In this picture, his hair was long and curly and his red cheeks shone brightly. Papa hated that picture and never would say much about it without using a curse word or two.

At some point during these singings in the original log room, Papa would get out his handsaw. This was a simple carpenter's tool, but in Papa's hands it became a musical instrument. Carefully, he would place the saw handle on the floor as he stood the saw up. His foot would hold the handle in place as he grasped the top of the saw. With his free hand he picked up his fiddle bow. As he created the proper tension by bending the flexible blade, he pulled the bow across the smooth side of the blade. The sound that came out was amazing. You could easily recognize each song as Papa expertly fiddled each song. Even today I cannot adequately describe the sound. The eerie melody produced by the handsaw cannot easily be described but must be heard.

As the tune of the Tennessee Waltz came from the handsaw, I sleepily lay on that linoleum floor in the front room of the Old House, surrounded by my family, and the music they loved. Laying there listening, I knew without words being spoken that I was in a secure place...surrounded by family as the warm glow of the fireplace illuminated the room. Even at this young age, I knew I was part of something very special and this was a good place to be.

I remember the night
And the Tennessee Waltz
Only you know how much I have lost
For I lost my pretty darling
The night they were playing
That beautiful Tennessee Waltz
-"The Tennessee Waltz" by Peewee King and Red Stewart

"Coco" Harper Lives

Recently, they built a new post office in Dry Creek. It's a large modular building complete with glass doors and modern conveniences. Out in front of it, the Postal Service poured a large concrete paving area. The whole setup is modern and nice; however, it just doesn't look like it fits in Dry Creek.

On the night after they poured the slab for the parking lot, someone slipped in and marred the still wet concrete. On the southeast corner of the slab, someone had written, "Coco Harper lives."

Therefore, it is my duty as an official Dry Creek historian to fill you in on the most mischievous resident to ever live in Dry Creek- Coco Harper. First of all, Coco Harper was not a person, but rather a spider monkey. He belonged to the Ryan Harper family who ran the grocery store where Foreman's Meat Market now stands.

Ryan Harper was a special person in Dry Creek. Known by practically everyone because of his country store, he was rough, crude, and very kind- all rolled into one larger than life man. Most of all, to me he was my friend. When an adult takes time to talk and listen to a child, that person will always be revered by the young person. Ryan Harper always had time for me when I went in his store. I never remember his being impatient with me as I visited at his store, and that is why he will always hold a special place in my heart.

I don't know what possessed Ryan and his wife, Iris, to buy a spider monkey. I guess it was to add to his collection of animals. Ryan lived across Highway 394 from the store and there was a steady stream of peacocks, chickens, and Doberman dogs roaming his yard and the store area. I believe the monkey was probably the idea of one of his two daughters, Ramona or Wynona.

The first time I saw Coco was sometime during the late 1960's. As I sat outside the store drinking a soda, Ryan's old two-tone blue Chevrolet Impala came driving up. I saw an unforgettable sight- there scampering back and forth on the front of the car was a skinny spider monkey. It was as if the car had a live hood ornament. This was my first, and definitely not last, encounter with this infamous monkey.

Wherever Coco was, he seemed to take over and when he was inside the store was no exception. Now I want to say this tactfully, but Ryan's store was not really well kept. I'll always remember venturing into the back room to get a case of Coca-Colas in the returnable glass bottles, and half expecting a bear to jump out of the piled-up junk and empty boxes that filled up the room.

My Uncle Bill, always quick with a quip, called it "Ryan's Rusty Restaurant." To me, Ryan's was a second home. Our post office was located at this time inside the store. Our postmaster, Mrs. Kat King, would let me look through the FBI wanted posters on the wall. In my young fertile imagination I half expected one of the criminals on the posters to come in the store door.

Ryan's store was a place where a young boy, by just sitting quietly and listening, could learn a great deal about our area, from the price of calves at the sale barn to the inside scoop as to why a deputy had to be called in to referee a spat between two neighbors.

I always felt at home at Harper's store. We had a charge account and I loved the thrill of getting a snack and saying, "Ryan, put it on our bill." My younger sister, Colleen, once exclaimed, "Momma, let's go get it at Ryan's, it doesn't cost us anything there."

However, when I selected my snacks, there was one area of the store I did not buy from and that was the cookie jar. Rumor had it that Ryan would sometimes let Coco stick his paw into the cookie jar and pick out his own cookie. I'm not too picky, but I didn't want a cookie that had been handled or smelled on by a monkey. Any way, as I remember it, those cookies were so stale, probably nothing but a monkey would have eaten them.

Coco Harper, as monkeys go, was pretty excitable. This led to a wild experience one day when Paul Young and I were in the store. Coco was sitting there on the faded green recliner that was the fashion statement of Harper's Store. Neither Ryan, nor the customers were watching, so Paul and I lunged at the monkey as if to catch it. Coco immediately went into a cataclysmic fit and began scampering throughout the open rafters of the store. Customers ducked for cover as the screeching monkey raced around.

Coco finally ended up going into adjacent post office. Mrs. King, the most proper lady in Dry Creek, came running out as Coco became the resident postal monkey for the United States Postal Service. (The fit that Coco threw, and also how Mrs. King reacted, would today be called "going postal.") Finally after a while, Ryan corralled the chattering monkey and a semblance of calm was restored. For some reason no one looked at Paul or me to ask what had set off this escapade.

Before you begin to feel too sorry for Coco, let me tell you what a thief he was. Once my friend L.D. Spears told of leaving his preschool son Greg and nephew Sean in the truck while he went inside the store to check his mail. When he came back out, there were the two young boys, petrified as they huddled together on the seat of the truck. There sat Coco, on the dashboard, eating the ice cream sandwich he had snatched from one of the boys.

Being a thief, Coco Harper was good at getting into vehicles and taking food. In Dry Creek, people never locked their car doors in this time before A/C was standard in cars and most folks left their car windows rolled down. This was all an enterprising spider monkey needed to stay fed.

Legend has it that Coco's favorite food was bread. He could rifle a loaf of bread and be gone with it quicker than you could believe. Bread was what led to Coco's most memorable adventure. Some members of Ryan's family were visiting at the Harper home. They parked their Lincoln convertible in the yard, and carefully put the convertible roof, or "ragtop" as it was called, up. They were returning from shopping at Piggly Wiggly in DeRidder, so their vehicle was loaded with groceries. Being fully aware of Coco's thieving ways; they wisely put up the convertible top.

Much to their chagrin when they came back outside, they found the monkey inside the car, enjoying a loaf of bread. The worst part was the long tear in the convertible fabric that Coco the burglar had ripped open to gain entrance to the groceries.

It wasn't long after that episode that Coco Harper disappeared from Dry Creek. I really don't know what happened to him, but rumors abounded as to his demise. My friend, Eddy Spears, who loved to tell a good whopper, told how a near-sighted squirrel hunter sent Coco to the Promised Land. Another popular story was how he was electrocuted while running along on a high line wire. Someone else said one of Ryan's Dobermans got him.

I never got around to asking Ryan what happened to his monkey, so I don't really know, but I've always suspected the man with the convertible was a good healthy suspect for the end of a memorable monkey named Coco Harper.

Yes, Coco Harper lives...but only in the memories of guys like me.

Playing Catch with my Dad

As I squat behind home plate, my dad readies his next pitch to the first batter of the inning. It is the late innings of a church softball game we are easily winning. I've come in from my usual spot in left field to let my son Clay play the outfield, while I catch.

Suddenly it occurs to me that it's been about thirty years since I've caught behind the plate for my dad. My mind goes back to my late preteen years when my softball-playing career began with the men's team. My dad always had a team that traveled around to play other churches and pick-up teams. Arriving at the ballpark, I always expectantly counted the heads of our players hoping that less than ten would show up. If they were short, it gave me an opportunity to play. They'd stick me behind the plate at catcher where I couldn't do too much defensive harm, and there I would catch my dad's pitches.

So here I am again, this time I'm over forty years old and still playing catch with my dad. What a privilege to be on the same team with both my son and my dad, and what a privilege to share this special love of baseball in our family.

Growing up, one of my favorite pastimes was playing catch in the yard with my dad. In those days dad still played fast pitch softball. As I got older, I became his practice catcher. He would throw a wide assortment of curves, fastballs, and knucklers that I would attempt to spear with my glove. Even as my hand burned, I gritted my teeth to prove to him I could catch his pitches. I believe he took great pride in testing me with his fast pitches, and I took it as an immense challenge to catch them.

All through the years, baseball has been a strong glue that bonded me to my father. Now as a dad myself, this wonderful game is something my three sons and I share that time cannot change. I cherish all of those afternoons spent in the yard with batting practice. Those hours of hitting grounders to the boys are some of the most precious times of my life. Games seen at the Astrodome or nights spent sitting together in front of the television, cheering on a game, are special moments that I will carry to my death.

I recall a story I once read about Harmon Killebrew, a Hall of Fame player with the Minnesota Twins. He related how as a boy, their neighbors constantly complained to his dad about how bad the Killebrew yard looked compared to the neighborhood's well manicured lawns. To make matters worse, the Killebrew lawn had a well-worn baseball diamond on it. His dad simply responded to the complaining neighbors with this comment, "We're not raising grass here. We're raising boys."

That's what I love about baseball- it is a game for fathers and sons to enjoy together. My favorite movie is "Field of Dreams." It is so much more than just a baseball movie. It is really the story of the relationship baseball can play in a father and son relationship. In it Terrence Mann, tells Ray, played by Kevin Costner, the following:

"The one constant has been baseball. America has rolled by like an army of steamrollers, been erased like a blackboard, rebuilt, and erased again. But baseball has marked the time. This field, this game, is a part of our past, Ray. It reminds us of all that was good and how it can be good again."

And it is good, and I'm glad I to still play catch with my dad, the major influence of my life.

A Saddle on a Pig... A Mercedes in Dry Creek

They no longer hold farm auctions at Pederson's Farm House north of Dry Creek on Highway 113. However, in its heyday no event could draw more people, and provide more fun, than these monthly auctions.

Because the main items offered for bids were farm-related, most of the people in attendance were country people. Any and every item imaginable would be offered for sale. Rumor had it that once an old stray dog wandered by, and they sold it for $5. Tractors of all sizes and makes, plows, old school buses, trucks, implements, and ranching tools all could be found at Pederson's.

And the daddy of this auction was Erik Pederson. Always dressed in his trademark wrangler jeans and brown khaki shirt, Erik looked the part of a real cowboy. Long, tall, always with a witty word and twinkle in his eye, Erik has always been one of my favorite people in Dry Creek.

Most of the Pederson auction clientele were just like Erik- country men dressed in their work clothes. Some came to see what they could pick up for this year's spring planting; others brought items to sell, wanting to see what price they could get. Then others were just there to look around, visit, and escape their wives' Saturday chores at home.

On the day of this particular auction in 1991, a unique item was brought to Pederson's farm auction. The day before the auction, two federal agents drove up in a new shiny white Mercedes Benz sports car. This car, confiscated from a convicted drug dealer, was driven into the muddy parking lot at Pederson's and parked right next to a 1952 Ford Tractor. There the Mercedes sat for bidder inspection, right among all of the farm implements.

One of the agents- non-smiling, wearing dark glasses, and standing there with his arms folded just like you see on TV, stood guard by the driver's door of the car.

Throughout Saturday morning, a steady stream of people lined up to inspect the Mercedes. The car's hood, trunk, and doors were opened so potential bidders could get a good look. The sight of this expensive luxury car sitting among the rusting older equipment reminded me of an old country saying. When someone would see something that looked completely out of place with its environment, the old timers would say "That's like putting a saddle on a pig!" To me, this luxury car being sold in Dry Creek is exactly what the "saddled pig" analogy implies.

As the line stretched longer, it reminded me of a boyhood visit to the State Fair in Shreveport. There, on display they had what was purported to be the "death car" of Bonnie and Clyde. A long line of people lined up, paid their dollar, and waited to put their finger in one of the hundreds of bullet holes in the car's body.

This Mercedes brought out the same interest in everyone here at the auction. Old men, who'd never driven anything that didn't have "Ford" or "GMC" on the tailgate, sat proudly behind the wheel of the Mercedes. As one man slid behind the wheel onto the plush white leather seat, the federal agent worriedly watched this farmer's bulging jaw full of tobacco and the brown stain running down his chin.

Country women, who didn't have enough in their checking account to buy a good brisket at Brookshire's, stared through the window as if they were figuring their bids and planning to take the Mercedes home tonight. Of course I was right in there among them gawking. One farmer was heard to mutter in disgust as he walked off. "Look at the spectacle of all of them staring at that car like a calf at a new gate."

This line of rural America continued throughout the morning. There was much good humor mixed with the gawking. Occasionally, there stood a lawyer or doctor, probably from Lake Charles or some other big city, lined up with all of the rest of the usual auction crowd. These men, dressed in their crisp white shirts and expensive suits, stood out from among Pederson's normal customers.

Finally the time for the sale of the Mercedes arrived. It was saved dramatically until the very end of the auction. Very few of the crowd left early, because everyone wanted to see how much this car would bring. As the crowd circled around stage, the bidding started. About ten well-dressed men, all strangers, actually took part in the bidding, as everyone else watched.

The opening bid was for $20,000. Way back in the crowd, someone whistled appreciatively. Bid by bid, the price surged upward. Gasps were heard when someone shouted, "$40,000." Eventually, a doctor from Lafayette bought it for $46,000. Slowly the large knot of observers walked away in groups or pairs. Many were shaking their heads in wonder at the idea of someone paying twice as much for a car as they'd paid for their home and land.

The rich bidders got in their Mercedes, BMW's, and Town Cars and went home. Pederson's normal clients loaded up in their trucks and headed home to Pitkin, or Longville, or maybe LeBlanc, and of course quite a few of us drove back down the road to our homes in Dry Creek. All had one thing in common- they had been witnesses to a memorable event in Dry Creek- the day they sold a Mercedes at the farm auction.

A few months later, I was in New Orleans riding the streetcar down St. Charles Avenue. We passed a Mercedes dealership, where row after row of these expensive German-made cars sat. A new one, white just like the one at Pederson's, pulled out into the street and stopped beside us at the next traffic light. I glanced around at the other streetcar riders, and no one even seemed to notice the Mercedes except me. I was once again reminded that I live in a place where some things, like Mercedes, are rare. I also live in a place that is just as interesting and fascinating in its own way as any large city any where. A place where so

Corporal Howard Vidrine

When I came to work at Dry Creek as a thirteen-year-old, one of the first people I met was Howard Vidrine. He served as the camp night watchman during my early years at camp. "Bro. Vidrine," as we called him, lived in the Evangeline Parish town of Reddell, which is next door to the unique village of Mamou, located in the deepest heart of Louisiana's Cajun country.

Forty years after I first met him at camp, Howard Vidrine is still a part of our camp family. In fact at the time of this writing, he is staying with us in his own personal cabin at camp.

The first thing I noticed about Howard Vidrine was his rich Cajun brogue. I love all Acadian accents, but there is something so different about the unique accent of Evangeline Parish residents. It has a character all of its own. I've always said if I was walking down the street in New York City and heard someone from Ville Platte or Mamou speaking, I'd recognize where they were from.

Bro. Vidrine is a bachelor, at least as I write this. Being eighty one-years old (Don't dare ask him his age) and pretty set in his ways, I doubt he'll find a wife at this point, but you never know. Throughout the years he has been a fixture at Dry Creek. A few years ago he moved into one of our small cabins as a special guest.

We never know when he is coming or going. He just shows up and that is always fine with us. He serves a very important role at Dry Creek Camp. He is the surrogate grandpa for several generations of campers and staffers. I guess that would be the best way I could describe the role he has played in my life.

Bro. Howard is an ordained Baptist minister. Several times he preached for us at our local church. I'll never forget the last time when he preached as to how he wore a big bow tie. I've found that anywhere I traveled in this part of Louisiana, he is well known. Once several of us went to check on him at his Evangeline Parish home, failing to find him there we found him at the local corner grocery. He told us this is where he came everyday to eat. It was neat how the young waitresses hovered over him as if they were serving royalty.

As I write this, I'm sitting by his hospital bed in DeRidder. He has had kidney stone surgery and is recuperating for a couple of days. During the last few weeks, our camp staff has taken care of him. Frank and Janet Bogard and the rest of our staff have always been so good to him and treated him as a grandpa to our staff.

During these last few weeks, I've had Bro. Howard tell me again about his wartime experiences during World War II. The men, who fought to keep our freedom during this most challenging war of all, are slowly but surely passing from the scene. It is important to tell their story for posterity. Here is his story:

Howard Vidrine volunteered for the Army in October 1942. He went to boot camp at Fort Benning, Georgia. He then took part in the Louisiana maneuvers held in Central Louisiana which were led by Generals Eisenhower and Patton.

Then he boarded a transport ship for the fourteen-day trip to Europe, his first trip very far from Evangeline Parish. They landed first in England where his division drilled for three months. Bro. Howard said "It rained every day we were in England."

Next, his unit went to North Africa to join the war in January 1943. His battalion, the 894th Tank Destroyers, joined the battle at Kasserine Pass. Corporal Howard Vidrine was in a reconnaissance platoon. Their job was to scout out and locate Rommel's tanks. Crawling along there in the Saharan desert sand he saw his first German tank. It was the first of many he'd see in the coming months.

This famous fight was a tank and plane battle between the Allied and Axis forces. It was during this time that the Mamou kid first worked along British soldiers. His main recollection was how they had their teatime daily at ten o'clock regardless of the conditions. He told me, "They really talked funny." I couldn't help but chuckle at him commenting on how they sounded.

His division pulled back after this battle. Bro. Howard told me a disturbing story of an incident that occurred during a later skirmish. The North African campaign was winding down as the Germans retreated through Italy. Howard was driving a jeep when he picked up an Italian civilian who was visiting his family in Africa. The Italian was so excited that his home country was being liberated. They continued toward town where they stopped and picked up an American correspondent. Upon nearing town they encountered German artillery fire and turned back. At this point the correspondent pulled his pistol and shot the Italian dead. Bro. Howard grimaced as he shared this story. He asked the American why he shot this man. The reply was "Well, he's the enemy, and he might have shot us." Over fifty years later, the pain of this episode could still be heard in his voice.

Next they boarded transports for the trip across the Mediterranean Sea to Italy. Landing at Naples they began their march northward. Upon reaching Anzio, Italy, they found no enemy. However, within a few weeks German forces began showing up with troops, planes, and artillery and the big battle began. Bro. Howard said he spent most of the battle in foxholes at outposts or on patrol.

He related another story that occurred during this battle: Bro. Howard and a lieutenant were on patrol. They went into a two-story house to check for Germans. They found no one in the house. The Germans were shelling the house with artillery. Therefore, they next went to a nearby cave where they spent the night with a group of civilians.

The following morning they went to a nearby field and hid in a haystack. Then they moved to a bomb crater and spent the day watching for German troop movement. By radio, they sent information telling of the Germans' location. The Allies were bombing with land artillery and guns from the ships in the harbor. The shells "fell like rain" as the barrage moved from the north to the south.

Soon, the German troops and tanks began moving right toward their fox hole. Over two hundred troops accompanied by a dozen tanks began approaching his position. Bro. Howard related as to how he had decided to play dead if they came upon his hiding place. When the Germans were within about one hundred and fifty yards, they stopped and pulled back due to the intense Allied shelling.

He also related the following story to me: While they were engaged in the battle at Anzio, mortar shelling went on all the time. One day as he left his foxhole during a lull, three fellow soldiers hollered at him to come over and join their card game. He replied that he couldn't because he had something to do. Within minutes, a shell landed in the foxhole killing all three men.

After the battle of Anzio was won, the Fifth army continued northward. During this time Corporal Vidrine had his one and only meeting with his commander, three-star General Mark Clark. As Vidrine was directing traffic at an intercession, Gen. Clark drove up, jumped out of his jeep, and asked for a light for his cigar. Corporal Howard Vidrine from Reddell, Louisiana, lit the cigar of famed General Mark Clark at this muddy Italian intercession.

The army entered Rome after its liberation. Bro. Howard commented on the friendliness of the Italian people. During this time he visited the Vatican and saw the Pope give his blessings to a large crowd at St. Peter's Basilica.

As they worked their way north, they came to the famous town of Pisa. Bro. Howard, when asked about the famous leaning tower, dryly commented, "Yeah, I saw it. It looked just like an old building about to fall down. It didn't impress me too much."

It was in Pisa that the war ended for Corporal Howard Vidrine. He was one of three men going to relieve two observers in a house. While approaching the house, they were hit by mortar fire. One man lost both legs, the other man had superficial wounds, and Bro. Howard received shrapnel in his shoulder and hand.

From there he spent a long time in military hospitals in Europe recovering from his wounds. He then began his journey back to Louisiana, never to venture far from home again.

To end this story, I'd like to share something that left a great impression on me. During November 1998, just after Veteran's Day, a delegation from Fort Polk visited our camp. They were looking at our facility for future staff retreats. They were led by Colonel Jason Kiamaya, commander of one of the regiments at Ft. Polk, our nearby Army base. Accompanying Colonel Kiamaya was Sergeant Major Clarence Harmonson, and two other men- the post chaplain and an enlisted driver. I took them on a tour of the camp and we had a good time walking and visiting.

As noon approached, we went to the dining hall for lunch. As we entered I saw Bro. Howard sitting at a window looking out across the campgrounds. Bathed in the bright sunlight coming through the window, he looked even older and frailer than his eighty-plus years suggested. Just looking at him in his simple clothes and weathered, wrinkled skin, there was nothing really physically impressive about Bro. Howard.

I pointed Bro. Howard out to Colonel Kiamaya and said, "See that man- His name is Corporal Howard Vidrine, a World War II veteran. He served with Gen. Mark Clark's Fifth Army fighting German tanks across North Africa and Italy. He was on the front lines of all of the major battles of that campaign. He received the Purple Heart after being wounded at Pisa, Italy."

As we neared the serving area, I called Bro. Howard over. He slowly shuffled over, dragging his feet as his house shoes made a scuffing sound. He hadn't shaved in several days and his clothes just hung on his skeleton-like frail body.

However, I was proud to introduce him to this group. Col. Kiamaya stepped forward, snapped off a salute, and said, "Sir, in respect and honor for you and your service to our country, I'd like you to go first in line.

Bro. Howard, being the humble (and stubborn) man he is, declined to go. However the Colonel, a man used to giving commands, would not relent until Bro. Howard went first. Therefore, with great deference, Colonel Kiamaya led Corporal Vidrine through the serving line first. I'll never forget the sight of the highly decorated officer walking behind Corporal Howard Vidrine.

We all sat together for the meal. The soldiers with their sharp uniforms, shiny medals, and insignia sat around Bro. Howard. It was with sincere appreciation how they listened and paid respect to this old man who had so faithfully served his country. The conversation around the table was special and made me, as a non-veteran, feel like an outsider. The camaraderie among these military men was both warm and real.

As I walked away, I glanced back at the green and khaki uniforms sitting in a circle of honor around an old World War II vet, a member of what is often called "The Greatest Generation." Here stood one living example of the men who rose up from the woods, plains, mountains, towns, and cities to join together to defend our American freedom during a pivotal time in history. The look on Bro. Howard's face did not look like a corporal in the midst of superiors. It was the look of a man among other warrior-soldiers, all united in their commitment to our wonderful country.

Epilogue: As I am putting the finishing touches on this story, Colonel, now General, Jason Kiamaya has returned to Fort Polk as the commanding general of the entire base.

Sergeant Major Clarence Harmonson recently retired as the highest-ranking enlisted man at Fort Polk.

Our special friend, Bro. Howard Vidrine, passed away at the Alexandria Veteran's Hospital in October 2000. He is buried in the very area of Evangeline Parish where he lived all of his life other than his war years. We miss him at Dry Creek Camp, but will always cherish his life and memory.

A Hog Dog under the Front Porch

Lloyd Iles with two of his hog dogs

When I was a boy, my grandfather raised woods hogs. These animals, in various stages between completely wild and semi-domesticated, were a passion of Grandpa Lloyd Iles. To raise, catch, and handle wild hogs, you needed help from another animal- and that helper was a good hog dog. Most of the dogs my Grandpa had were just curs- a motley mix of Catahoulas, hounds, and maybe a touch of pit bull. There was one thing they had in common- an inborn instinct to go in the woods to corral and catch hogs.

Papa kept them in a pen or they would've stayed in the woods all the time. When you'd look at them in their pens, they were a sorry-looking collection. The Catahoulas, with their pale blue glass eyes and fierce dispositions, in one pen, and the "brindle" dogs [that is a brown dog with darker stripes across his back.] My grandpa always said, "A brindle gyp (female) is the best hog dog you can find."

This unusual mix of mongrels was lovingly cared for by Papa. He treated his dogs with great respect and love. The fence around the pens, to keep the dogs in, looked like pictures I've seen of concentration camps. There was wire everywhere. Even above the top of the fences was a horizontal section of wire to keep the dogs from leaping over the six-foot high fence.

However, these dogs weren't prisoners, instead they were honored guests. My Grandma Pearl always made fun of how well Papa fed his dogs, but she knew the reason he loved them so- They helped him do what he loved best- hunt and catch hogs in the swamp.

There were over one hundred hogs in the woods with the Iles mark. The grown hogs were marked on their ear with the family mark, which differed from the other woods hog owners. This marking was done when the hogs, preferably in the piglet stage, were caught and brought to the barn. There they were marked and the males were castrated. You have never heard more squealing than on the day when these small pigs were marked.

The majority of Papa's hogs were pretty tame and stayed near the barn and house. He fed them each evening at dusk. One of my favorite childhood memories was to hear Papa hollering his hog call, which sounded like a cross between a yodel and a rebel yell. As the hogs noisily came running up, he'd toss shelled corn to them. It was a sight to behold, and solidified the saying, "eating like a hog" in my mind.

But these semi-domesticated hogs were not the ones which intrigued me the most. The truly wild ones that lived deep in the swamp away from the intrusion of humans were the ones that both fascinated and scared me.

On journeys into the woods, I would occasionally come upon these wild woods razorbacks. With caution I'd carefully watch them. If there was a sow with piglets, I'd give them an especially wide berth. I'd also carefully watch the large boars. When I encountered them, with their huge protruding tusks and high ridge-backed hair, I'd always scout out a nearby blackjack tree to climb if needed.

There was something truly free and remarkable about these animals. Their fierce freedom and isolation deep in the woods really made them seem even more admirable as they lived on their own, far away from humans. During the time of my childhood, our community was in a time of great change as fences were being built, land was being posted, and forest land was being converted to soybean fields. It was very obvious the era of hogs, cattle, and sheep running loose in the woods was coming to an end.

I think that freedom is also why Papa enjoyed these wild hogs so much. The truly wild hogs, found only deep in the swamp, represented the spirit of wandering freedom that he admired. The wildest hogs were the ones he hunted with his dogs. . .

On the day of a hog hunt, even before he opened the dog pen door, I believe the dogs would sense what was about to happen. There they'd be—barking loudly, tails wagging, and jumping at the fence.

When the actual hunt began, it was something special. We'd go down into the swamp where the acorns were thick like carpet on the ground. This is where the dogs would usually find the wild hogs. The dogs would chase the hogs until they finally surrounded them. This seemed to always end up in the thickest briar patch around. The barking, squealing, and sounds of battle still ring in my ears a generation later.

The sight of a large hog held down by three dogs- one on each ear and another on a leg- was something to see. I know in our politically correct age this sounds kind of cruel, (I hope you remember that Jimmy Dean didn't invent the sausage you enjoyed for breakfast this morning!) Our meat has always come from animals- whether wild or tame

Anyway, the hogs weren't killed right then. They were driven back to the barn by the dogs. The sight of trained dogs herding a dozen squealing hogs through the woods was a sight to behold. The shepherding instinct of these dogs was fascinating to watch. Finally, this barking and squealing sideshow would end up at the barn, where the hogs were driven in through the gate, penned up, and fattened over the next few months, until ready for butchering.

Often during these hunts, hogs would scatter everywhere, and the dogs would individually go after them in every direction. Many times when the hunt would end, successful or not, several dogs would be missing. This never seemed to worry Papa. He simply commented, "Oh, they'll be home sooner or later."

Many times it would be several days before old "Jezebel" or "Ringo" showed up at the Old House. There were times when I'd given up on ever seeing one of the missing dogs again. Then, up the road he'd come. Limping and tottering badly, much skinnier with ribs showing, and tongue hanging out. For all practical purposes, this dog looked to be on its last legs. A closer examination revealed cuts and scratches from the hogs, briars, and underbrush. The pads of the dog's feet would often be scraped and bleeding from running in the woods for no telling how many miles.

Papa wouldn't even bother putting this worn out haggard dog in the pen. He'd just allow it to crawl up under the high front porch of the house. A bowl of water was placed there with some food. Sometimes the dog was so whipped; he wouldn't even eat for a day or so. He'd just lay there, head on his paws, sleeping the day away, licking his wounds when awake.

Then one day, sometimes maybe two or three days later, I'd look out and there the same dog was- padding across the yard, tail wagging, good color back on his gums and a healthy look in his eyes. It was amazing how this dog that seemed down for the count was on his feet again and ready to go.

As I look at the busy schedule we live, I think about that hog dog under the porch. We live hectic, fast-paced lives that leave us exhausted, cut, and whipped. From being out in the swamps of life, lost and without direction, we often find our way back bleeding- not from our feet or wounds, but something far worse- wounds in our souls and spirits.

But sadly, we do not follow the instinctive wisdom of these dogs. Instead of taking time to recuperate, rest, and lick our emotional wounds- we rush back out and enter the barking, squealing fray again- only to later return more exhausted.

Then we act surprised when our body breaks down, or our soul feels dry and malnourished. This fast pace of our life, full of so much excitement and adrenaline-producing activities, fails to really satisfy.

For too long we Christians have ignored our leader Jesus' model of ministry and renewal. No one was ever busier than our Savior during His earthly ministry. However a careful reading of the gospels, reveals what my friend Stan Allcorn calls, "Jesus' model of intense ministry interspersed with regular periods of retreat, rest, and renewal."

Mark 1:31 illustrates one example of this in Jesus' life: "Very early in the morning, while it was still dark, Jesus got up, left the house and went off to a solitary place, where he prayed."

When one of these hog dogs, which had been busy doing what it was created to do, returned home it took time to rest, before returning to its normal routine. This rest was needed for renewal and recharging for future hunts.

When we ignore this God-inspired need to rest, it is a sin. God had a perfect reason for His commandment, "Thou shalt keep the Sabbath holy." He gave this commandment for our protection and benefit. Our human body is created to need this rest. When we ignore God's law, we sin, and sin always results in pain. When we think we are "Superman" (or Superwoman), and ignore God's guidelines, we are only heading for a crash. The only question is will it be physical, emotional, or spiritual, and how long before it happens.

Because Jesus went hard in every way- socially, spiritually, emotionally, and physically (remember he didn't rent a chariot for those long walks in Galilee.) Because of this, he wisely took planned breaks from intense ministry. Examples throughout the scripture bear this out.

Once again, we best heed Jesus' example. I'm amazed at how many people, nearly always men, proudly exclaim, "Why, I haven't taken a vacation in eleven years." First of all, that's pretty dumb and doesn't sound like very much fun, either. We need extended breaks from the jobs we love, and the pressures of everyday life.

One of my main hobbies is hiking. When I go on a backpacking trip in the mountains, a strange feeling of peace gradually settles over me. Each day I am outdoors, it seems to grip me more securely. This feeling of peace, a serenity of the soul, helps me to see things as they really are. Perceived problems, with seemingly impossible and insurmountable obstacles, all shrink back down to their normal small size. While out walking, tough and knotty decisions just seem to loosen and untangle themselves.

A Latin proverb sums it up best,

Solvitur Ambulando: "The difficulty is solved by walking."

During these times of retreat out into nature, a quietness comes over me where once again I can hear God's still, small, and powerful voice in my soul.

Returning to the real world of ringing telephones, deadlines, and multiple responsibilities, it doesn't overwhelm me because I've had this time of retreat, rest, and renewal.

It is important to remember that we must control our time or it will control us. It's much easier to respond to the urgent call of the hundreds of voices calling us for our attention, than to have the self-discipline to build times of rest and quietness into our lives. Real life, and real peace, come from coming apart where those interfering voices recede and God's voice resounds in the silence of our soul.

"Come apart or you will come apart."
Vance Havener

A Dry Creek Haircut

Once when my son Clay was seven, he came home and announced, "Daddy, today I got my hair cut by a man." I could only shake my head in wonder. I wondered how *old* I was before a woman cut my hair. I've always felt uneasy having women cut my hair. It probably has a lot to do with my upbringing. Any man from my generation in Dry Creek is probably the same way.

Just last week, my dad who is sixty-seven years old told me, "Well, today I did a first. I got my hair cut by a woman." He'd broken down and went to Kathy Deshotels' In Style hair salon. There's one major reason why most Dry Creek men my age or older never had a woman cut their hair-That reason was Pete Harper's barbershop.

Pete Harper, who lived in the nearby Shiloh community, was a circuit-riding barber. By this I mean he cut hair weekly in Reeves, Longville, and every Monday in Dry Creek.

When I first started getting sheared by Mr. Pete (I use that word "sheared" literally, Pete's one style was a crew cut.) he was located in Elliott's Store across from the old Dry Creek School.

I was so small that I sat on a board placed across the chair. Years later as an older teenager, when I got my last Pete Harper haircut, he was still favoring the close cut haircuts of my preschool years.

Later Pete moved his shop to a small white building located south of Ryan Harper's store. In addition to being the local barbershop, this 10' by 10' building was our local polling place. When election time came, they simply pushed the barber's chair out of the way and brought the one voting machine in.

On Mondays, all of the boys needing haircuts would get off the bus at the crossroads by the shop. It was always a race between our bus (south Dry Creek) and Monette

Lindsey's bus (west Dry Creek). If you were the last one off the bus, you had a long wait ahead of you ... so the competition was stiff getting in line to stake your spot, then to await your turn in the chair.

As soon as we staked our place in line, we'd rush over to the store for a Coke and Moon Pie, or a bag of chips. After purchasing these afternoon snacks, everyone returned to rightfully find their place in line.

As we gathered in the small shop, the conversation was loud and interesting as boys with their mouths full of food related to Pete the events of another school day. Talk of school, basketball, and hunting filled the air as the clippers whined and clumps of hair fell to the floor.

The older boys told of the "good old days" at Dry Creek School when they could leave school, climb the stile over the fence, and get a Pete Harper haircut during the school day. That sure sounded good to my young mind as I sat waiting my turn, when I'd rather been home playing.

As everyone crowded into the small shop, some boys would sit on the small homemade bench in the corner. Others would stand around, leaning against the walls, as they awaited their turn.

Some boys would go outside where often trouble would occur. Once, one of the older boys peed in a cream soda bottle and got several of the smaller boys to all take a swig. After that episode, my mother made me promise on the pain of death not to be outside unless the barbershop caught on fire.

Back inside, Pete would pop the cloth apron to remove any hair, and say, "Next." I never remember any arguing or disagreement over the order. The next boy would jump up and take his seat in the chair. Soon there would be a good cross-section of Dry Creek hair piled on the floor... mainly dark brown with a few tufts of blonde mixed in, and a patch of red hair, when Wesley Farmer or one of the Miller boys was there.

As he cut, Pete would tell story after story about his days in the Coast Guard, or basketball games won in dramatic fashion, or a recent trip he'd taken to Houston where he related about all kind of strange people he'd seen. When he'd reach a good part of the story, he would stop cutting and hold the buzzing clippers as he emphasized a point. If you were the occupant in the chair at this point, it was a nervous time as the clippers buzzed back and forth by your ear. I also never recall, in all of Pete Harper's stories, any ugly language or off color remarks. He was funny and entertaining without needing to be vulgar.

Besides the stories, there were many rituals involved in a Pete Harper haircut. His first question was always, "Do you want it with bangs hanging down in the front?" This was during the 1960's when every self-respecting boy in Dry Creek had a crew cut or "butch" as we called it. The Beatles may have been the rage, but no Dry Creek boy would dare have bangs or hair over his ears. To have worn your hair like that would have been open to great ridicule, mainly coming from men the age of Pete Harper.

Pete would always add, "If you have bangs, you've got to wear pink panties." To this day when I see a man sporting bangs, I immediately think of those pink panties. That is just one example of the influence of this man, and his barbershop, in my life.

Pete Harper had one way of cutting hair: close-cropped, marine style. You always left there knowing you'd got your money's worth and never wondering if you've had enough cut off to please your parents.

One of the wittiest guys who ever grew up in Dry Creek was Mike Barrett. Mike, the brother of Jimmy and Don Barrett, always had a funny story for every situation. I didn't personally witness this event, but Freddy Roy Atkinson did and related it to me.

One Monday, Mike, then a teenager, stepped up to sit in Pete's chair. Pete said, "Mike, how'd you like it cut today?"

Mike's reply was, "Well Pete, I'd like it cut short on the left side and leave it longer in the back. I want this sideburn left longer than the other. Then I'd like the front gapped up."

With a puzzled look, Pete said, "Now Mike, I can't cut your hair like that."

Mike's quick reply was, "I don't know why you can't, Pete. That's how you cut it last time I was here."

Two other stories come to mind and my dad figures in both of them. During the late 1960's, my dad, as most men his age, hated the longer hair that was coming into style. His favorite saying was, "When you turn eighteen, you can grow your hair as long as you want, but for now, you'll keep it short.

Eddy Spears was my good friend. Eddy always had long hair that hung down in his face when he leaned over. My dad liked Eddy and worked with him at church, but always worried about his long hair and how "he'd like to have gotten some scissors on it."

Once when Eddy's parents were away on a trip, he came to stay with us. It was Monday and I needed a haircut (at least according to my daddy). He took both Eddy and I to Pete's barbershop. He told Pete, "Give them both a good crew cut." Eddy protested mildly, but we both left the shop with matching crew cuts. I know it had to be the crowning achievement of Pete's long career to get those clippers on Eddy's long stringy hair. I've always wondered what Eddy's parents thought when they first saw his new hairstyle, courtesy of my dad and Pete Harper.

The second haircut story involving my dad occurred several years later. The fads and changes of the 60's had finally found Dry Creek. Boys were now wearing their hair longer, bushy sideburns were in vogue, and the lines weren't as long on Monday afternoons at Pete's shop.

I was about fourteen and as I plopped down in Pete's chair, I instructed him, "Leave it longer on the sides." To my dismay I left the shop with the same old short butch haircut I'd always gotten.

Years later, when I was in college, Pete told me this, "Curt, your dad came in and said, 'Pete, that boy of mine is going to come in and want one of those long-hair hippie haircuts. Just give him a crew cut no matter what he says. It's my two dollars and not his.' So Curt, I was just following orders from your dad."

Maybe that was why after several of these short haircuts in a row, I rebelled and refused to go back to see Pete. Soon I began going to DeRidder for those fancy razor cuts. Later I backslid to places where they even wet your hair before giving you a haircut. Eventually, I ended up on the prodigal road to the long hairstyles of the seventies and to shops where I let "Delilah" actually cut my hair.

Never again was I to hear the drone of the clippers as dark brown hair cascaded down the front of the apron. No more would I feel the warm shaving cream and straight razor as Pete Harper shaved the back of my neck. Gone was the talcum powder shaken on with a horsehair brush.

However, in my memory the sights and sounds still remain. The sweet mint-flavored cologne that was the finishing touch of a Dry Creek haircut by Pete Harper. The butch wax that made your remaining hair stand up in front.

Sometimes in my mind, I still leave the small barbershop and start my four-mile walk home. I know that I won't have to walk far before someone will pick me up. This is my hometown and everybody knows each other. As I walk, the cool air of a passing car reminds my ears of how much shorter my hair is now than it was an hour ago. Then my Grandpa Lloyd pulls up beside me in his 1961 white Ford. As he opens the door to let me in, he grins and says,

"Looks like you've been to see Pete Harper." We ride home visiting, the air from the open passenger window blowing in my face.

I don't remember exactly when Pete Harper closed his shop in Dry Creek. The small white building is long gone. I believe it's in Arthur Crow's front yard where it serves as a tool shed. We now vote at the old school. Pete is retired and has moved to DeRidder. The days of Pete Harper's barbershop are long gone. From time to time, I still see Mr. Pete, and when I see him, I think to myself, "There is a very rich man. He is a man with so many friends and so many stories- how could such a man as this be considered anything but wealthy?"

No Man Can Serve Two Masters

Most days I carry my dog, Ivory to work with me. When she sees me lower the tailgate of the truck, she begins dancing excitedly. Ivory is a large yellow Labrador Retriever. She really belongs to my son Clint, who bought her five years ago. Because I spend a lot of time with her at work, I like to pick at Clint and say Ivory is really my dog. He quickly reminds me that he is the one who paid good money for her, and therefore she belongs to him.

At the camp, Ivory loves to sit outside the door of whatever building I'm in. Faithfully, she waits in the shade for me to come out. The only exception to this is when I enter the Dining Hall. No matter which of the seven doors I enter, she quickly goes to the side door where campers exit after meals. She has learned this door is the prime spot to beg scraps from campers.

When I leave the Dining Hall and don't see her, I give my Grandpa's hog dog call and she comes running around the corner of the building- full of camp biscuits and ready once again to be my faithful companion.

Recently, Clint and I walked out of the camp office together. As we exited outside, there was Ivory grinning her silly smile, as she expectantly thumped her big tail against the wall. I challenged Clint to a test, "Clint, let's stop here and find out who Ivory really loves the most. You go north to the road and I'll go east to the Tabernacle. Whom she follows will show her true allegiance." He reluctantly agreed to my challenge. I was confident she would follow me because of how faithfully she always follows me each day.

We both agreed not to look back until we had walked to our respective spots. As I walked the seventy-five feet to the Tabernacle, I expected at any time to hear the sound of her steps behind me. I held off looking for as long as I could. Reaching the sidewalk I stopped, and looked over to

Clint. He had also stopped at his spot, the same distance from our starting point, but Ivory had followed neither of us. There she sat right where we'd left her, anxiously looking back and forth from one of us to the other. She excitedly wagged her tail and moved her front legs as if to come to one of us. Then she resumed her looking as if she was saying "Eenie, Meenie, Miney, Moe...."

Then as we approached each other, Ivory left her spot and ran to us, arriving just as we met.

I felt guilty for putting her in such a tough position. I promised Clint that I would not bother him anymore about whom Ivory loved best. She evidently loved both of us equally.

The words of Jesus came to me as I thought about Ivory's allegiance. Jesus clearly stated that no man can serve two masters. In the Sermon on the Mount, he clearly spoke of allegiance and dedication,

"No one can serve two masters. Either he will hate the one and love the other, or he will be devoted to the one and despise the other. You cannot serve both God and money." Matthew 6:24.

In this case Jesus compared serving God or worshipping money- Which is a good illustration because most of us find this decision to be a tough one. However, no one should congratulate themselves too much because all of us have at least one major area that appeals to us, yet blocks our relationship to God.

The scariest part is this: many times, we stand and look back and forth at which master we will serve. The other object drawing us away from God is often something good, but anything that blocks our communion and dedication to God is harmful, no matter what it is. We must not settle for good when we can have the best- a close intimate relationship with Jesus. Jesus meant it when he said we can only serve one master. I saw this very principle in a humorous, but dramatic, way recently at Dry Creek Camp.

One of our joys at camp is planning events for folks to attend. Most of the time during the year we host church groups of all types. On many of these weekends we will plan events, such as ladies retreats and couples events, for folks from various churches to attend.

Recently, we scheduled two separate events for the same weekend. At our Adult Center we held a couples retreat. This is always one of our favorite events. Couples arrive Friday evening, tired and frazzled from a busy week. Beginning with the evening meal, we pamper them and take care of every need they have. There is always a couple who leads this program of marriage enrichment. Our Adult Center allows these guests to mix and learn together while at the same time giving each couple needed privacy to be together away from the demands of their busy lives.

These couple's events are attended by a wide range of folks. Most of the couples are young, but we will have one or two older couples, sometimes in their sixties or older. Just like the younger ones, they are here to learn more about making the coming years of their marriage the best yet.

Among our couples there are always a few who qualify as "eager wives/reluctant husbands." I can spot them quickly; the men look as if they are there for a public hanging- their own. Usually as I sign them in, the husband will whisper to me, "Now, this wasn't my idea, but to keep the peace I came." Or they'll reveal a bribe, "She told me if I'd come to this, I could go fishing at Toledo next weekend."

The neatest thing to watch is how over the weekend, many of these "reluctant husbands" enjoy the retreat best of all. They relax, make new friends, laugh, and enjoy falling in love all over again with the woman they married.

As the couples arrive in the dining hall for the first meal, we make sure they all sit together and meet other couples. Soon a magical sound starts. I call it the "sound of fellowship." Here's how it sounds: It begins as a low buzz as people begin to visit, and it's accompanied by the sound of silverware clinking. Soon, a new sound enters this symphony. It's my favorite Friday night sound- the sound of laughter. It lets us know these strangers are beginning to come together as new friends as they relax in the special environment that occurs at camp. I firmly believe this sound of fellowship is used by the Holy Spirit to lay the foundation for the spiritual victories to be won tonight and throughout the weekend.

After the meal, the couples walk in small groups back to the Adult Center, better known at Dry Creek as the "White House." Because darkness has now fallen, we hand out flashlights to each couple. I always enjoy reminding them that there had better not be any kissing or hanky-panky on the trail back to the White House.

Then the first session begins. I like to quietly sit in the lobby and just listen. We are blessed with great leaders who know so much about marriages and have the ability to present it in a creative and fun way. I've never seen a Friday session that didn't have eruptions of hearty laughter all evening.

Sometimes as the couples share, it sounds like the old Newlywed Game from the 1970's. Listening carefully, the loudest laughter seems to come from those reluctant husbands. I silently thank God for what He is doing in the lives of these precious couples. I'm also thankful we have a facility to minister to these adults. Our passion and priority is reaching young people, but when we can be a part of seeing God strengthen marriages, we are equally thrilled. Anytime marriages are strengthened, everyone wins.

Now, I want to tell you about our other event of this same weekend. Each year in February we sponsor a one-day "Turkey Hunting Seminar." This event is planned and carried out by one of our retired employees and special friends, Joe Watson. I jokingly refer to Joe as our "head turkey."

This Saturday seminar has grown into a well-attended event. During the entire day, these dedicated hunters get together and "talk turkey." They have calling contests, go to the rifle range to pattern their shotguns, and trade stories all day long. Turkey hunters are among the most passionate of all hunters and the men, women, and young people who attend, are no exception.

They bring stuffed turkey mounts, turkey decoys, calls, pictures of prize birds, magazines, and anything else that has anything to do with turkey hunting. One year, our area's best hunter, C.W. Caraway, brought the beard and tail feathers of his state record turkey. Everyone reverently gathered around as if the Hope diamond was on display.

In addition, we usually have a local taxidermist bring several mounts of various animals. Often, Mark Atkinson will set up one of his hunting stands in the Dining Hall. By the time the seminar gets going, the room is filled with excited hunters and paraphernalia of every type.

One thing all of these hunters have in common is their apparel. Every person, even down to the smallest child brought by his dad, is outfitted in camouflage. Turkey hunters are experts at hiding themselves from this intelligent and wary bird. Every camouflage pattern known to man is modeled on this day.

Walking into the dining hall, there is so much camo and surplus army clothing that you'll wonder if you've stumbled upon the annual convention of one of those radical militia groups from Montana. However, the best part of this event is the spiritual emphasis throughout the day. Several of our turkey hunters give devotions from God's word. They use analogies from hunting to share the gospel and the power of God. We are always thrilled at the number of unchurched folks who attend this event. Anytime, we can invite people on to our grounds and share with them concerning the great love of God, is always a great opportunity.

One year Ricci Hicks, a hunter from Longville, shared a devotion using his calls and gear. His talk was entitled, "How Satan deceives men." Using each of his hunting items and techniques, he really brought home about the methods the devil uses to attack men.

On this February Saturday morning, the turkey hunters fill up one end of the dining hall as they meet, laugh, learn, and drink our coffee pots dry. As we get ready for lunch on the other end of the Dining Hall, it never enters my mind as to the conflict we are going to have in this Dining Hall in a few minutes.

Soon our couples group, after finishing their morning session, will be coming to the dining hall for lunch. After their meal, they will return to the White House for one final afternoon session on this Valentine weekend.

So, get this picture. In fact, I know some of you are even ahead of me. Standing on one end of the dining hall is a group of sixty camouflaged turkey hunters. On the other side of that very front door are twenty-five couples ready to come in and eat. It had never even entered my mind about the conflict that this would create.

As soon as the couples came in, I knew we had trouble. The first expression I saw of it came from one of my favorite couples, Kevin and Cathy Willis. Kevin is one of my best friends in the whole world. As I shared earlier in this book, he is my duck hunting partner and fellow deacon. He is a big burly man with a heart as big to match his body. He is passionate about anything he does- singing, hunting, being a good dad, and especially following Jesus. However, when he comes through the door and sees all of the hunting stuff spread throughout the dining hall, he looks as if he is going to be sick. This is the expression of a man who loves the outdoors and hunting and has just discovered how he has missed the opening day of hunting season.

His wife Cathy's face is just as passionate. As Kevin gazes longingly at the hunting gear, Cathy has the same look of a woman who sees her husband ogling a younger woman. She is ready to try to drag him away from temptation and back to the White House.

Most of the couples there have the same kind of reactions to some varying extent. Every country man worth his salt likes to hear about hunting and see camouflage, whether he likes to hunt or not. As the couples begin going through the serving line, several of the men comment to me concerning my lack of foresight in putting a couples' retreat and hunting seminar on the same weekend.

Kevin wants a vow from me, "Bro. Curt, please promise me you won't ever schedule another couples event on turkey hunter's weekend."

I try apologizing to these men from the Valentines Couples' Retreat. Finally, I give the only comment I can think of, "Sorry guys, but no man can serve two masters."

Although this story is humorous and probably slightly exaggerated, (that's called "literary license.") the principle behind it is serious, when we attempt to serve two masters, we will be completely miserable.

As the couples leave the dining hall, some of the husbands look back longingly with the same gaze I imagine Lot's wife had as she looked back on Sodom. But I hope they realize the joy that comes from sacrificing what you **want** or enjoy for **someone** you love. There is a great difference between these two and much of our happiness and fulfillment in life comes from right choices between things and people.

Yes, Jesus hit the nail on the head. We cannot serve two masters. Just as Ivory whined at being unable to choose between her two masters and my hunting buddies were torn between their wives and camouflage, we are most unhappy when we are in the no man's land of attempted dual allegiance.

Sometimes, the most miserable person in the world is not the person who has no room for God in their life. Yes, that person is unhappy and unfulfilled. However, there is probably no worse spot to be in than attempting to be both a follower of Jesus and the world. May we constantly be reminded of the love and grace of Jesus. Let us never forget His strong call for us to forsake this world and our own wants to wholeheartedly follow Him, this Amazing Jesus, the Son of the Living God.

"Then choose for yourselves this day whom you will serve...
...but as for me and my house, we will serve the Lord."
Joshua 24:15

The Lights of Houston

To me every hour of light and dark is a miracle,
and every cubic inch of space is a miracle.
Walt Whitman

This week at camp our guests are from the Houston, Texas area. This is their twenty-sixth consecutive year to come to Dry Creek. We love them deeply and always enjoy the week when all four hundred of them visit us. These city folks really enjoy being in our rural environment. In every activity, they seem to inhale every bit of our fresh clear air as they soak in the sights and sounds of a week of camp in the country. I remind myself that they can teach me not to take for granted the simple, but priceless, gifts we enjoy in Dry Creek.

This is especially brought to my attention by a comment from one of the men from Houston. On the second day of camp, he tells me, "I love this week each year. It is the only time I ever get to see the Milky Way." I'd never thought about this, but I know from past visits to cities how the vast number of lights and smog obscure all but the brightest objects in the night sky. I recall a sign I once saw in a rural Texas general store:

"Life is too short to live in Houston."

On this week of camp, the last remnants of Tropical Storm Allison have finally shifted eastward, leaving up to three feet of rain in some areas of Houston. Here in Dry Creek, we escaped these heavy rains, which claimed over twenty lives in Texas.

There is at least one benefit of a tropical storm or depression: the strong weather system pulls much of the humidity and vapor with it as it tracks north. This leaves clear beautiful skies, which are ideal for viewing of the stars and planets. Tonight is that type of night. The moon is in its last quarter and doesn't rise until later in the night. I walk out into my backfield at home as darkness falls. As my eyes adjust to the darkness, the vast multitude of stars seems to explode forth and cover the canopy of the heavens.

The entire sky is covered with glittering stars. In the eastern sky I see the planet Jupiter; to the south I see the constellations of Scorpio and Sagittarius. As always, I look for Polaris, the North Star. It's not bright, but glows faintly in its special solitary place in the northern sky. Rotating around it is the Big Dipper. Finding the front two stars of the dipper, I make a straight imaginary line across the sky to find the North Star.

Overhead the Milky Way, our galaxy spreads across the sky. Estimated to contain several hundred billion stars in addition to our star, the sun, it is only one of an endless number of galaxies in the Heavens. This vast chain of stars, stretching across our night sky, is so vast that it takes the light 100,000 light years to travel from one end to another. [4]Basically, the Milky Way is too big for our finite mind to comprehend.

Standing outside, my eyes begin to adjust to the night light and the vast array of the stars seems to explode forth. In addition to my eyes, my ears pick up the many sounds of the night. I first notice the song of the crickets in the trees. From different directions, frog choruses, on three surrounding ponds, attempt to drown out the competing frogs in the other bodies of water. It is a beautiful sound that always represents the warmer time of the year. Finally, mosquitoes, another product of the milder weather, begin biting my legs so I leave the night sky and go back in the house. Inside I search for one of my favorite quotes from

---

[4] Matthew 6:24

the Indian leader, Chief Seattle, when he visited with President Franklin Pierce in Washington in 1855:

"There is no quiet place in the white man's cities. No place to hear the leaves of spring, or the rustle of insect wings. What is there to life if a man cannot hear the lovely cry of the whippoorwill or the arguments of the frogs around the pond at night?"

It is so true that we Americans seldom get where it is really quiet. In fact, true silence and solitude seem to make us uncomfortable, when in reality it should relax our mind.

Yes, summer nights are great for enjoyed the sounds of nature. Summer is also good for stargazing, but the best time to view the night sky is in winter. It's cooler, the humidity is lower and the sky puts on a show with the brightness and magnitude of billions of stars.

The winter constellations are different from the summer sky. In the southern sky I find my favorite constellation, Orion the hunter. It takes a little imagination, but I can see why the ancient sky watchers thought this group of stars represented a mighty hunter. He is accompanied by his two hunting dogs, Canis Major and Canis Minor. His dogs wage an eternal fight with Taurus, the bull. These constellations, and many more, are spread out across the southern part of our evening sky.

On cool evenings, I go outside to relax under these same stars after a busy day. I drag an old rusty metal cot out in the field, and on it I throw a faded cotton mattress. Lying on this springy bed, I look up and soak in the beauty of stars and the quiet solitude of the moment.

Soon, my dogs come to join me. Eddie, our feisty little rat terrier, jumps up unto the cot beside me. Ivory, our yellow lab, patiently licks my hand and calls for my attention. But my eyes aren't on either dog because the allure and beauty of the night sky has all my attention.

Other than the years I was held as a prisoner of war in the city where I attended college, I've always enjoyed these rural night time views. I never tire of this special privilege of enjoying God's great creation as seen in the sky.

The majesty and classic simplicity of Genesis 1:1 is never clearer than being under the stars on a country night. "In the beginning, God created the heavens and the earth."

Recently, I heard evangelist Sammy Tippit share about a trip to Russia. While walking across the campus of a university, he went up to a young man and began a conversation. When their subject turned to God, the student stopped and told Tippit the following story:

He shared, "You're probably going to think I'm crazy, but I must tell you this story. All of my life I have been an atheist. My parents are atheists; my teachers have all been atheists. But last week, as I stood outside on a beautiful starry night and looked up into the Heavens, I realized for the first time that there is a God. There is no way our expansive universe could have just occurred by accident."

The student continued, "Right there, I prayed for the first time in my life. I told God, 'If you really exist, as I think you do, prove it by sending someone to tell me about You.' So, here I am standing with you. Tell me about God, I'm ready to listen."

Sammy Tippit emotionally shared about telling this young Russian about Jesus, the Son of God. This man- who knew nothing about God either spiritually or intellectually- saw God's fingerprints all around him and became a believer.

Yes, as I look up into the Heavens and consider the intricate clockwork of our universe, I always wonder why anyone would doubt a Creator when looking around at His handiwork.

Sometimes as I lay on that old cot, I'll track a satellite moving across the sky. In another part of the sky, the blinking lights of a jet slowly pass overhead. The plane is probably six miles high and zooming along at hundreds of miles per hour. However, due to my perspective, it is a tiny slow-moving blinking light among thousands of stars.

Many times in the cold of winter, the coyotes will begin howling in the nearby edge of the woods. Although I'm not far from the house (and I'm not a scaredy cat,) I begin moving toward the house, as the coyote howls seem to grow nearer. Every dog within earshot of our house begins barking fiercely in response to the coyotes. Returning to the warmth and safety of our house, it feels good to be back inside.

Some nights I'll be fortunate enough to be present for meteor showers. These events, which occur like clockwork each year, happen when our Earth, making its yearly orderly orbit around the sun, passes through the debris trail of a comet. The debris, dust, and rocks, left centuries before by this comet as it made its orbit around the sun, remain on its long path across the universe. This space debris burns up as it enters Earth's atmosphere. These chunks and pieces of rock are what we call meteors. These meteors, or "falling stars" as we commonly call them, streak across the sky. Most of these particles are minute and not very bright. However, from time to time a large meteor, or fireball, will streak across the sky. This sight, very similar to a fireworks rocket going across the sky, will sometimes break apart into trailing parts, and is a sight you won't soon forget.

This love affair with the night sky has been a lifelong passion for me. I recall one very special time in my life. I was teaching physical science to freshmen students that year. My students were not the college-bound levels, but they were grouped together to work under me. I was determined as to how we would learn together and have fun while doing it. My goal was to make the subject matter interesting, and learn as we applied the information of science to our everyday lives.

When we came to the study of astronomy, I was excited because it is fun to teach about an area you love. In addition, I quickly discovered how my class also loved studying the stars, constellations, planets, and the clockwork appearances of the sun, moon, and comets.

Soon they began reporting to me things they'd seen in the night sky. They were quickly getting hooked just as I was. It was so neat to draw out a constellation on the chalkboard, then tell them where and when to look. The next day they would excitedly share their discoveries.

To close out this study we took a nighttime field trip to McNeese State's observatory east of Lake Charles. The bus was loaded because country kids always enjoy a road trip. They also knew the "Curt Iles rule of bus traveling"- we always stop at a fast food place to eat. (If they gave the driver a free meal!) To us country folks, "eating out" is a big deal.

At the observatory, the large telescope was trained on the planet Saturn. It was a clear dark night and Saturn and its rings showed up brilliantly. One by one, the students peered into the large telescope. I stood to the side where I could see their expressions. It was great to see the look of wonderment come over their faces. Some of them just wouldn't leave the eyepiece for others to have their view.

I especially enjoyed the reaction of some of the more cynical boys. One of them rubbed the eyepiece with his hand as if he could rub the painted-on Saturn off the lens and expose this optical trick. Several more climbed up the steps near the large front end of the telescope. I believe they were trying to get up there to see if some contraption or image was attached on that end.

Finally, they were convinced what they saw was truly Saturn. Next, we observed Jupiter and watched its moons orbiting around the huge planet.

As we left the observatory, they found Saturn and Jupiter in the night sky. It was so special to see how differently they now looked at those far off pinpricks of light.

I tell this story to share this: Many of those same students, now young adults, still live in our area. They are all over thirty and raising families. But from time to time, one will come up to me, once again with the bright eyes of a fourteen year old and say, "Mr. Iles, did you see that meteor shower last week" or "Have you seen how bright Venus is right now each evening on the Western horizon?"

Just like my students, I observe the wonderful clockwork and majesty of the heavens, I am still amazed. How anyone can think this is all by accident sure has more "faith" in this universe being accidental than I do. I see the handwork of God as I observe the regularity of earth's rotation around the sun and the cyclic phases of the moon. The earth is set at just the right angle on its axis, and spinning at just the right speed, to create and maintain temperate weather for life to exist. Any drastic changes in this tilt or our rotational speed would mean temperature extremes that would make life impossible.

When I read one of my astronomy books and see where they can correctly predict, decades ahead, the exact day, and time of future solar or lunar eclipses, I'm amazed at the clockwork precision of our universe and the great God who created it.

Yes, the night sky speaks to me of the glory of God. I'm reminded of David's words in Psalms 19, "The heavens declare the glory of God; the skies proclaim the work of his hands."

In addition, I think about the bright lights of Houston and how there are folks who've never enjoyed standing with the one they love under the starlit night sky on a clear country night. I'm sure those folks think we miss many of the benefits of city living. But, I think just the opposite-what could be better than living where you know your neighbors, and you don't have to always lock your car, and best of all, walk out in your backyard and see the vast array of stars stretching across the skies.

"I'd rather sit on a pumpkin and have it to myself, than to be crowed on a velvet cushion."
Henry David Thoreau

A Broken Pencil

La Esperanza, Honduras

I stood in muddy water in the middle of what was now a raging stream. Only an hour ago this spot was the middle of a dirt road on the side of a hill in northwestern Honduras. We arrived here at the home of a family to set up our video equipment and screen to show *The Jesus Film.*

Upon arrival a few hours before dark our team, consisting of missionary Billy Capps, Randy Pierce, my son Clay and I, was met by a group of smiling dark Honduran children. Setting up our screen and tarps, we kept an eye on the sky above the surrounding mountains. It was May and that meant the beginning of the rainy season in Central America. So we worked hard on our tarps to have them ready for a storm, should one come.

While we waited for dusk and a crowd to gather, we showed the children witnessing beads and bracelets that explained the plan of salvation. As I tied a bracelet on a dark eyed boy, I laughed as I recalled last night's service when we ran out of bracelets before the Honduran pastor's elderly mother received one. The intense Spanish of the pastor to our interpreter, Alexis, didn't have to be fully understood for us to realize his momma badly wanted a bracelet, too. We dug in our bag in the truck and found the black, red, white, and yellow beads. I was out of leather strips so I improvised one with a rubber band and the old woman gave a contented toothless smile as I placed it on her wrist.

Tonight, we've come with plenty of bracelets and leather strips. We are happily handing out the beads and trying to explain their significance. Alexis, a young seminary student and our interpreter for the week, is using the microphone and amplifiers to invite the surrounding settlements to attend and see the video.

If you aren't familiar with *The Jesus Film*, let me briefly tell about it. It is a two-hour production, based on the gospel of Luke, that simply shares and shows who Jesus is- from his birth to his resurrection. Produced in 1978, it is extremely well acted and professionally produced. It is widely used the world over and has been viewed by an estimated four billion people. *The Jesus Film* is available now in over 273 languages.

Tonight's language, of course, Spanish. Alexis continues his invitation to attend, and to my English ears it is as if a machine gun is shooting out his staccato Spanish. As Randy Pierce sets up the large screen and adjusts the video projector, DVD player, and generator. To test everything, Randy begins the film. He chooses to use Chinese as the language for this test run. Here we are in the mountains of Honduras, watching Jesus speak Chinese, with the subtitles also in the same language.

As dusk approaches, a small crowd of forty or so has gathered. Most perch on benches in the roadway or sit with us along the ditch bank. Off in the surrounding darkness I can make out the forms of people, mostly men, who will not come closer, but sit at a distance under the trees.

As the film begins, every eye is on the screen. We are miles from any electricity and I wonder if any of these folks have ever seen a movie. The quietly humming generator runs the DVD player as the light of the movie reflects off the rapt faces of the Hondurans.

I shift my seat on the bank and pull out my bag of corn nuts. My new friend, Leonel, who has come with us nightly, grins appreciatively as I fill his hand with the delicious salted nuts. Suddenly, on the other side I feel a body snuggling up to me. I turn to see a precious girl, whom I'd met earlier, holding her hand out for corn nuts too. I recall that her name is Denise and gladly pour corn nuts into her little eight-year-old hand.

She munches contentedly and snuggles closer to me. We've each found a new friend, and it doesn't really matter to me that our friendship is based on my corn nuts.

The movie continues. Just about the time that Jesus stills the storm on the Sea of Galilee, the first raindrops fall. Then a clap of thunder introduces the real rain and the bottom drops out. Everyone runs for cover under the two tarps. Within minutes the road is running inches deep in water. The wind blows rain in on the huddled women, boys, and children. Our tarp, though secure, is holding water in a low spot and we work hard periodically dumping the water out before it collapses on the people.

Finally, after about twenty minutes of raining hard, it slackens. By now Jesus is on His way to Jerusalem. It's still raining hard but not nearly as hard as it was earlier. I slip to a drier area under the tarp and sit on a log. Settling down I feel someone snuggle next to me on my right side. I'm not really surprised to see the smiling face of my friend Denise. She nods yes as I extricate the corn nut bag from my rain jacket. She crunches contentedly as our gaze returns to the screen.

Then, on my left side I feel the warmth of another human body. A Honduran woman is sitting beside me. It's very dark but I can make out her smile and tell her hello, as I return my attention to the film. On the crowded log we are tightly packed and I feel the woman's body against my shoulder. From her side smacking sounds distract me, and with my eyes now adjusted to the darkness, I see that this Honduran mother is nursing her infant child, oblivious to this embarrassed Yankee seated next to her. My only thought is, "I sure am a long way from home here!"

Finally, through an hour of steady rain, the film ends. *The Jesus Film* features a wonderful invitation at the end giving each viewer the opportunity to invite Jesus into their life. Alexis stands in the rain and issues a call for all who've made this decision to come forward. From back in the crowd a young boy steps forward. Soon there is a small group of teenage boys who came forward one by one. They are being soaked as they stand in the pouring rain, but it doesn't look as if they really care.

As long as I live I will have the picture in my mind of these seven boys gathered around Alexis as he prays with them. They had made a decision to come to Jesus and were going to do whatever it took to receive him, regardless of the rain or what anyone else thought.

Then I recalled the story of the four men in the second chapter of Mark's gospel who brought their lame friend to see Jesus. Finding Jesus in a crowded room teaching, they went to the roof and after cutting a hole, lowered their friend to the wonderful Savior. They had a "whatever it takes" attitude to bring their friend to Jesus. Isn't that exactly what we should have concerning the Savior? There is no distance too great, no weather too bad, no obstacle too large, and no wall too high. Whatever it takes, we need to bring others to Jesus.

This night reminds me of how we in America really don't know what commitment and sacrifice are about. Here are people who've walked miles to see this film. Some of them are willing to stand in the pouring rain to show their desire to follow the amazing Son of God, Jesus. After the film, many will make long walks in the dark and up slippery muddy mountain paths as they trudge homeward. It humbles me as to how I take so many things for granted and often do not really show gratitude for my blessings.

During our time in Honduras an event occurs that leaves a deep impression on me, even to this day. Here is what happened:

At camp in Louisiana we use various objects to communicate the gospel as we share with young people. Mike Paxton, pastor of First Baptist of Kinder, is one of the best at using these objects to illustrate a point.

One of the best illustrations he uses is called "The Sin Trap." Mike takes a big rat trap and decorates it with glitter and fake jewels. On the bottom of the base he has written "sin trap." As he is talking to youth, he is holding the baited trap which is also set and ready to snap shut.

A big eight-inch rat trap is powerful and could probably break your finger. Mike deftly handles it. He pulls a pencil out of his pocket and begins to poke the baited area with the pencil. All the while he is telling about how Satan makes sin look so inviting, just like that morsel of cheese looks good to the rat. Mike continues, "Furthermore, Satan will let you play around with sin until you get comfortable and then he'll get you." Mike then springs the trap, which loudly snaps the pencil in two.

It is a memorable lesson that gets the attention of youth and communicates the message that there is always a price to pay for sin. As my son Clay and I prepare for our trip to Honduras, I make my own sin trap. I hope that with my limited Spanish, this visual lesson will help them understand. The only difference on my trap is that on the bottom I inscribe: "Pecado trampa," which means "sin trap" in Spanish. Additionally, I put several pencils in my pack.

While in the mountains of rural Honduras, we stayed in the home of Southern Baptist missionaries Billy and Betty Capps. Each night we would travel to one of the nearby areas to show *The Jesus Film*. Billy Capps drove a Toyota four-wheel drive truck that could go anywhere. We nicknamed the truck "Lottie Moon," because the money used to buy this truck came from the annual offering we Baptists take for the needs of our missionaries. The offering, taken at Christmas, is named after one of our earliest and greatest missionaries, Lottie Moon of China.

On our second day in Honduras, I showed Billy Capps my sin trap. At the end, I impressively sprung the trap and the pencil loudly broke in two as one end flew across the room. As Billy nodded at my exhibition, I could tell he wanted to tell me something, but was hesitant. Then he kindly told me, "That is a great lesson. However, if you willingly break a pencil in front of these people, they will be very disturbed. You see, most of them have never had a pencil of their own, and it would really upset them to see something so precious purposely destroyed."

I was so embarrassed and ashamed… Here I was, having done this little trick over and over with numerous pencils and it never even entered my mind how wasteful I was being. Needless to say, I didn't use any pencils with my sin trap. It was just as easily done with a small stick. It was very effective as I told them about Satan's schemes and strategies, the whole time being interpreted by one of the young men with us. The snapping of the trap always elicited an excited response and I believe the lesson was conveyed.

However, the most important lesson was learned by me. Here was something I thought nothing of- a measly pencil, but to these people it was a treasured prize. I thought of how many pencils are probably in my house. I know every time I look under the couch or recliner, there are several. Yet, here I was, so ignorant of these people and their needs.

Since that trip I've shown the sin trap many times. Nevertheless, never have I, and never will again, willingly break a pencil.

God, help us in America not tot be so wasteful and thoughtless. We have so much and appreciate it so little. Teach us to have gratitude for all that we have.

"To whom much is given, much is expected."

I can wholeheartedly recommend Macedonian Missions and my friend, Randy Pierce. This ministry serves to link volunteers on work projects and *Jesus Film* trips with Christian missions in Central America. If you'd like more information, contact www.macedoniamissions.org

The yearly Southern Baptist Lottie Moon mission offering takes place each December. All funds given go to directly meet the needs for over 5000 missionaries worldwide. Go to www.imb.org to receive more information on how you can give and pray.

To find out more about The *Jesus Film*, contact their website at www.jesusfilm.org.

Heavenly Treasures on Casino Road

The silver BMW zooms by me as we head west on US 190 outside Reeves, Louisiana. It's a hot Saturday afternoon in June, and as always, our Louisiana summer humidity is tough to bear, and impossible to enjoy. I'm driving the camp van, loaded with a dozen sweaty and laughing boys, and the AC doesn't work very well. We've got the windows cranked down, but it's still just plain sweltering inside the vehicle.

But the heat is probably not bothering the two occupants in the BMW. Their darkly tinted windows are tightly shut. As the car speeds around our slow van; I'm not at all surprised to see the Texas license plates above the rear bumper.

US 190 is what we call the "Texas Casino Road." It is used by the multitudes of Texans who come to our fair state to gamble at the Grand Coushatta Indian Casino, north of Kinder.

This shiny new luxury car is in stark contrast to what I'm driving- a 1978 Ford van. In addition to being hot, this van still bears evidence from yesterday's canoe trip - the lingering aroma of wet bathing suits and soured towels, and some of the remaining creek sand on the floor is being whipped up by the wind and stinging our eyes.

I'm sure our Texas friends, who've just passed us (if they even noticed us at all) thought we were a pretty motley crew. This van has seen many miles, first carrying foreign seaman from the Port of Lake Charles, and now hauling kids to and from camp.

As this luxury car quickly puts great distance between us, I think, "Well, I wonder how they did at the casino? Are they going home happy- with more than they brought- or like most visitors, are they leaving with pockets empty and broken dreams from a weekend which they had hoped would be profitable?"

Then I recall a story. (It seems everything makes me think of another story!) It's one concerning a Texan who bragged after returning to Houston from a weekend at the casino. "Boys," he said between puffs on a big cigar, "I went over there in a thirty-thousand dollar car and came back in a three-hundred thousand dollar bus!"

. . .The only part he omitted was that this bus was a Greyhound Bus. This funny story is a sad reminder of the troubling practice as to how casinos will quickly loan you more gambling money in exchange for your vehicle title.

As my mind contemplates this and the silver BMW puts distance between us, one of the boys in the van hollers and my eyes are diverted back to the rear view mirror. It is important to keep a check on these campers I'm taking home to Lake Charles. These are Opportunity Camp boys. They've come to camp because their parole officer sent them. Some came to camp as an alternative to juvenile jail time, while others have come because their parents were more than happy to have them gone for three days. Regardless of their reason for attending, they've all had a great time and been model campers during the three days of camp.

As I glance again at them in the rear view mirror, I don't see criminals, or a certain race, or any hate- I simply see young boys who've had very little guidance, spiritual or otherwise, in their lives. Boys who need male guidance and involvement. Boys who, most of all, need the life-changing love of Jesus in their lives. I recall how many of them, including most of these six, made first time decisions to follow Jesus as Savior, Lord, and guide of their lives while at camp.

Returning my attention to the road, I recall a thrilling experience from the last night of camp. After our evening service a camper came up to me. He asked, "Are you a counselor here?" There was an urgency to his question that riveted my attention on his dark brooding eyes.

"No, I'm not really one, but how can I help you?"

"Man, I want Jesus... and I want Him now!" he blurted out. As we went outside and sat at a picnic table, it was my privilege to be there when he asked this Jesus to become real, forgive him, and come into his life. I'll always remember his simple, crude, heartfelt prayer:

"Jesus, you know I done a lotta wrong in my life, and there's a whole lot of forgiving I need, but I know you can, and will, save and forgive me."

I've been with many young people when they've reached this decision to get to know God's Son, but I've never heard anyone pray more earnestly and passionately, than this young man.

As the van bounces along in the rutted lanes of US 190, I recall other neat stories from these three wonderful days of camp. What a joy it is to be part of God's life-changing work at Dry Creek Camp!

Looking ahead down the highway, I can barely see our Texas friends in their BMW. They are now only a distant speck. Then the thought hits me and I really believe it is from God- even if these Texas travelers hit the jackpot and are returning home filthy rich, they aren't nearly as rich as I am. Here's why: I'm hauling a van full of new Christian young men. Who knows, there might be a preacher sitting behind me, or one of those three sitting in the back seat may mature into the kind of Godly man who will break the cycle of heartbreak and sin that have marked his family for generations.

A verse comes to my mind from Jesus' words in Matthew 6:

Do not store up for yourselves treasures on earth, where moth and rust destroy, and where thieves break in and steal. But store up for yourselves treasures in heaven, where moth and rust do not destroy, and

where thieves do not break in and steal. For where your treasure is, there your heart will be also.
(Matthew 6: 19-21)

You see, the only things going to Heaven are people's souls! Nothing else will make it, not even one single dollar of all the casino jackpots ever won. I think of the words of Mr. Leonard Spears, "Son, I've lived here on the road to the cemetery all of my life, but I've yet to see a hearse drive by with a luggage rack."

Therefore, when we view life with an eternal perspective, we realize our earthly possessions are temporary and will be someday left behind. Therefore, we need to be busy storing up heavenly treasure while we are here on earth- the everlasting treasure of investing in the lives of our greatest resource- young people.

Yes, our *business* is to be busy about His *business*. As Jesus said, "I've come to seek and save that which was lost."

Yes, I wouldn't trade these "heavenly treasures" laughing in the back of the van for anything material this world has to offer. Because in the long run, *and the eternal view is always the long run,* the things that matter aren't "things," but people.

As the popular MasterCard Ads say, "Certain things are priceless." And being part of God's life changing work at summer camp is priceless...and eternal... and worth doing whatever it takes to be part of.

What good will is it for a man if he gains the whole world, yet forfeits his soul?
Jesus as quoted in Matthew 16:26

Wings and Roots

I wrote this during a two-week hiking trip in the woods of Maine. Each day as I walked through the beautiful untouched forests and stopped beside the vast lakes, I had plenty of time to reflect. It is amazing as to how, after about three to four days of walking and living out in nature, your mind just clears and things and events come to visit you in the freshly cleaned recesses of your mind.

I believe the combination of being two-thousand miles from home, coupled with being in the outdoors for this extended period that were the seeds of the story I'm going to share with you.

My first reaction to the mountains, as I climb up and look across the vista of ongoing forests, blue skies, and the nearby surrounding majesty of the mountains, is one of awesome wonder. When I'm walking in the mountains, I always break out into my favorite hymn, "*How Great Thou Art.*"

When thro' the woods and forest glades I wander,
And hear the birds sing sweetly in the trees;
When I look down from lofty mountain grandeur,
And hear the brook and feel the gentle breeze.

Then sings my soul, my Savior God to thee;
How great thou art, how great thou art!
Then sings my soul, my Savior God to thee;
How great thou art, how great thou art![5]

During those days of walking, climbing, and worshipping, I thought much about my family- both present

---

[5] *How Great Thou Art* Swedish Words, Carl Boberg 1886 Translated English words, Stuart K. Hine 1949 Copyright 1955 by Manna Music

and past. During these days of wandering and wondering, the unique contrast between my two grandpas kept coming to me and this story began to evolve, first in my heart, and then later in the small notebook I carried.

They say you're the product of your genes. And I believe there is a lot to that notion. I'm the oldest grandson of two men who passed their genes and traits into my generation of siblings and cousins.

There have probably never been two men more different than my two grandfathers- Lloyd Iles and Sidney Plott. All that mattered to me was how they had one thing in common- they very obviously loved me and I loved both of them greatly, and still do, with an undying love and devotion.

My Papa Lloyd, my dad's father, was a "Dry Creek Man" if ever there was one. He was happiest being in Crooked Bayou swamp, raising livestock, growing the tallest corn around, and simply being at home. He never showed much inclination to roam about. Except for a short stint at Louisiana State University, and a miserable year working at a bank in Oberlin, he never ventured far from his birthplace in the woods.

A favorite family story, told best by my Uncle Mark, concerned several members of the Iles clan once going on a trip to New Orleans. As always, every trip east required a stop in Kinder to visit Uncle Dan and Aunt Lydia Iles, my grandpa's uncle and aunt. On this particular trip, the group included my grandparents and several of their children. Upon arriving at Uncle Dan's house, they got out of the car. They were greeted at the front porch by Uncle Dan and Aunt Lydia. My grandmother announced the family's destination as New Orleans.

Aunt Lydia stood on the porch with her arm on the railing. She looked at my Papa and chirped, "Lloyd, are you going too?" Papa turned to Uncle Mark and snorted under his breath, "She thinks I'm a dad burn hermit!"

Whether he was a hermit or not, he definitely preferred staying in Beauregard Parish. Born and reared on land homesteaded by his grandparents, he grew up following his grandfather daily through the fields and woods. He learned the art of hunting, growing a garden, fishing, raising hogs, and just enjoying the simple life. In her memoirs, his wife, my grandma Pearl, told about how after dropping out of college to return home to the woods, Papa was given a job by his uncle at a bank in Oberlin. His stay there was short. The call of the woods, just like the call of an owl in the stillness of the night, lured him back to the only life he wanted- living in the country.

However, while in Oberlin something good did happen- he met my grandmother. They were soon married and shortly before moving back to Dry Creek, their first son, my dad, was born. This family of three moved back into the old house, which was already inhabited by Papa's parents, grandparents, and an old maid aunt.

I always wondered about the shock of my grandmother moving into this house full of three generations. Mama always spoke happily of those days surrounded by these folks who quickly made her part of the family.

So my Papa, Lloyd Iles, returned to this environment he loved, surrounded by the woods and family. He had deep roots and he saw no reason to pull them up. It's probably no coincidence that I grew up next to that same old place and still live just a few miles away.

My Papa Iles gave me roots and a deep sense of belonging, family, and kinship with the land. For me he modeled a love for nature, the woods, and outdoor living that I inherited from him. He loved living close to the earth, and was a very earthy man- direct, no pretense, and grounded in what he wanted to do.

One thing he worked hard at was getting out of work. I don't mean he was lazy. He worked hard at keeping the old house, fields, and woods, taken care of. However, any day job he had, whether a paper route or as the parish registrar of voters, was only to help him get by so he could do what he wanted back in Dry Creek.

He was ingenious at attempting to find an easier way to do any chore. The best example of this is what I walked up on once in his back yard. I rounded the corner of the house and saw one of the most unusual sights I've ever seen: Papa had his horse, Dallas, hooked up pulling a lawnmower. He was holding the reins on the horse as he walked along beside Dallas.

That was funny enough, but to add to the spectacle there was my grandma Pearl, who had been assigned the job of guiding the mower by pushing it.

Another story related to me concerned the deep friendship he shared with his closest boyhood friend, Bruce Heard. They grew up as classmates and hunting companions. My Papa was a very good shot with a rifle or shotgun. Once, his friend Bruce helped demonstrate this accuracy.

Bruce put a lit cigarette in his mouth and walked about twenty yards away. He turned sideways where Papa could get a side profile of the cigarette and Bruce's face. Papa took his .22 rifle and shot the end of the cigarette off as Bruce Heard stood stock still, in complete faith in his friend. I've always thought that episode was pretty stupid on both ends, but it does say a great deal about the trust and friendship these two boys shared, as they roamed the woods together.

Yes, my grandpa Lloyd was a man who loved the country and its way of life. Even though he's been dead for nearly thirty-five years, I remember him well. That is one of the wonderful things about grandparents- they live on in our memory, throughout our lifetimes, long after they are gone.

An example of this occurred recently. I was in the post office when I encountered Mr. Leonard Spears. Mr. Leonard is well over eighty and one of the patriarchs of our community. As you read earlier, his family was one of the earliest settlers of Dry Creek. He was also a great friend of my Papa.

On this recent day, as Mr. Leonard and I visited in the foyer of the post office, I could smell the rich aroma of the Cotton Boll tobacco he had in his mouth. It'd been years since I smelled it, but its unique odor immediately took me back to my Grandpa Lloyd, also a faithful Cotton Boll chewer.

To anyone else the smell of chewing tobacco would not be very appealing. But to me it was a direct link to my childhood and family. When the old-timers got a chew, they would "cut off a plug" with their knife. I was amazed at the amount of tobacco some of the older men could stuff in their jaw. Cotton Boll was by far the most potent form of the chewing tobacco brands. I personally found this out once when I "borrowed" some of his tobacco. I didn't get a big plug, but I got enough to make me sick and cure any desire I had to follow Papa's example as a Cotton Boll chewer.

Yes, my Papa Lloyd was a country man from his head to his feet.

Now my mom's dad, "Grandpa Sid," as his three spoiled grandchildren called him, was much different from my other grandfather. This was especially true concerning roots.... He was born in Kansas City... From there I couldn't even begin to tell of the all the places he lived. From Illinois to Missouri and then finally to Louisiana. He and his family lived a life of moving up and down the

Kansas City Railroad line from Missouri to Beaumont, Texas.

Grandpa Sid was a railroad man, as was his dad, uncles, and brother. I've always heard about railroad blood getting inside of you. It's a desire to be on the move and see new things, and my grandpa evidently had it. He met my grandmother, Leona, at a boarding house in Hornbeck, Louisiana where she lived with her own grandmother. My grandpa was a young telegrapher at the local depot. After their marriage, he and my grandmother continued on their journey of moving from depot to depot, town to town. As time went on, they had three children, the youngest being my mom.

They lived in DeRidder, Louisiana long enough for my mom to meet my dad. Soon they were on the move again, leaving behind their youngest daughter and her new family.

As my Grandparent Plotts neared retirement, they settled in Shreveport, Louisiana. Even after they "settled" down, the call of the road still was there.

They continued to travel all over the United States. My Grandpa Plott was a great horseshoe pitcher and went every year to the World Horseshoe Tournament. He was the Louisiana State Champion for over fifty years.

Sidney Plott

My Grandparents also spent a great deal of time coming to see us, because my two sisters and I were their only grandchildren.

We always laughed when they brought jugs of Shreveport water on their visits to Dry Creek. The idea that anyone would prefer that chlorinated, chemical-laced water over our deep well water was preposterous to my sisters and me.

We also laughed just as hard, when several years later, they began bringing empty milk jugs from Shreveport, then filling them with Dry Creek water to take back to Shreveport.

I believe I inherited "railroad blood" from my grandfather, directly through my mom who has never met a trip she didn't like. Many times as the freight trains noisily moved through the nearby community of Reeves, I envisioned myself jumping up into a boxcar and seeing where this train was headed. During the still mornings waiting outside for the school bus, you could often hear the rumbling of the train in Reeves, over ten miles away.

Nevertheless, even if I had been brave enough to jump a train, I know it wouldn't have been long before I longed to be back home, in Dry Creek with my family.

You see I have a mixture of wanting to stay in the place I call home and wanting to see new things and have new experiences. This tug of war pulls strongly in my heart day after day. The wonderfully frustrating tension of loving where I am at against the passion to see places I've never been.

So, as I sat there on a big rock in the middle of a cold mountain stream in northern Maine, I realized how much I had to be thankful for. I thanked God for both of my parent's families. I thanked him for each one of my grandpas.

There is a saying: We should give our children two things- give them wings and give them roots. Thank you, my beloved grandfathers, for each of you giving one of these two things to me- one who gave me wings to fly, and the other who gave me roots to always return to.

A Man's Touch, A Man's Tears

Just as I turned to go out the front door of Foreman's Grocery, there stood "Jocko" Willis right in the doorway. I hadn't seen him in several years. As we saw each other, we met together in a big hug and just began visiting right in the doorway. There are some friends that when you see them, no matter how much time has elapsed, you just seem to pick back up your friendship, and he is one of those friends. It was a joy to see them.

As Jocko and I visited, we stood close together. He had one of his big strong arms on my shoulder. Jocko was especially concerned about my dad, who at that time had just been diagnosed with cancer. My dad, Jocko, and I had all played hundreds of softball games together.

We spent several minutes just sharing. As we hugged goodbye, there were tears in both of our eyes. As I turned to go to my truck, I looked back inside the store and saw three people at the checkout counter just gawking at Jocko and me. It really tickled me at their reaction to two country men publicly showing outward emotion with a hug and tears. I laughed as I though what Jocko, a big strong hard-working man, would have done if any of these strangers had questioned his manhood.

That's what I'd like to talk about in this story- The subject of men, their emotions, and being able to freely express our feelings to those we love. I've seen over the years a slowly emerging and healthy openness where men are not afraid to express their feelings.

I was once again reminded of this journey of openness later the same week after my visit with Jocko. Another Dry Creek native, Conrad Green, dropped by the camp office to send a fax (we have one of the few fax machines in Dry Creek.) As one of our ladies faxed the information, he and I just stood by the door and talked. He told me stories of my great grandpa and we laughed as he shared some of the milestones in Dry Creek's history.

After a good while, there was an uneasy silence. I knew I had to say it, so I decided to plunge right in, "Conrad, I sure think about Jeff a lot."

Conrad quickly replied, "You think about him? Why, I think about him every day!"

He said this in a kind yet emotional way. I could tell it was both painful and soothing for him to hear Jeff's name.

Jeff was Conrad's youngest son. In the fall of 1999, Jeff was severely burned in a refinery accident. After an agonizing time of hanging in the balance between life and death, Jeff died.

I had been Jeff's teacher, and later, his principal. He was always one of my favorites - A real Dry Creek young man- tall, robust, big enough to cause trouble had he wanted to, but possessing the kind smile and even-tempered personality that made everyone love him.

As Conrad and I looked at each other, I put a hand on his shoulder. Then we began talking freely about Jeff. We told funny stories about Jeff and laughed together. Then in the next sentence, there were tears in our eyes. There was nothing I could do to take away his pain of losing a child, but I wanted Conrad to know I remembered Jeff and still cherished his sweet personality.

I've learned that people want to know that a deceased loved one is remembered. Often we will not bring up the name of this loved one, because of the fear it may cause tears and sadness. But families need to know, from others outside their kin, how their loved one is still remembered.

Over the years I've kept a simple calendar in my planner. On it is recorded the birthdays and anniversaries of my many friends. In addition, I record the important dates of those I love who've passed away. One of the hardest things to do on a birthday, anniversary, or death date is to pick up the phone and call a family member. It seems as if the phone weighs ten thousand pounds. However, I call anyway because I'm learning the call is worth the risk.

While talking, I simply look for an opportunity to say, "Today is a special day for you, isn't it?" Then I hear over the phone, or see with my eyes, a combination of sorrow mixed with the sweet memories of a loved one.

It's much easier to say, "I'm not going to call them on this date. It will make them sad." But, I've learned without exception the words said in reply to my call is, "I've thought all day about him. I'm so glad that you remembered too." You see, we don't make them sad by remembering, instead we give the wonderful gift of knowing they, and their loved one, are very special to us.

I'm glad the fax transmission is taking a long time, so Conrad and can continue visiting. We have the neatest conversation, and I'm so glad I mentioned Jeff's name.

I think of times when a family has lost a loved one and because of the pain of grief, they never really address it as a family. Soon, it becomes as if the person never existed. He, or she, is on everyone's heart, but no one speaks their name to avoid upsetting the others.

Continuing to address the death of a loved one is important, and my sweet visit with Conrad reinforces this belief. As he leaves we hug, and I realize this will be a memorable day for both of us because of this time spent visiting. Heading back to my desk, I'm reminded of how many things I have to do today. But nothing I do the rest of this day will be as important as my visit with Conrad.

My encounters with Jocko and Conrad remind me of how important it is for us as men to express our feelings with words, emotions, and even tears. This is not a sign of weakness, but rather a sign that we are alive deep down in our soul and heart.

As I consider this art of what can be called "the manly hug/touch," Kevin Willis comes to mind. As you may recall from earlier stories, Kevin is a member of our church and also my duck-hunting partner. Best of all, he is just a very special friend you can depend on to be there as needed.

He is a Godly man and a very consistent follower of Jesus. He's a big strong robust man- about 6 foot 2. He works for a timber company managing their pine plantations. He's never been afraid of work and approaches everything in life with an excitement and passion.

He is a "man's kind of man." When you see him, you'd better get ready because you're going to get a great big old bear hug. After one of those hugs you'll wish you had a flak jacket on as your ribs recover from one of his lovable hugs.

Now, Kevin is a very emotional man who cries at the drop of a hat. It may be as he talks about one of his three children, sees a beautiful sunrise over the rice fields, or when he sings at church. However, there is nothing weak about Kevin. He reminds me that real strength is always found in gentleness.

I'll remember until my dying day how Kevin called me every day during a difficult period of depression in my life. Each day at some time, whether he was in the woods on a cell phone, or at home that night, he took time to check on me. He didn't talk very long, but he always reminded me of his prayer support and left me with encouraging words.

I'll never forget this "manly man" who reaches out to so many folks in our community. Kevin's big and rough hands are the hands of Jesus. Through his hands, hugs, and even tears, he "touches" many people.

When I see paintings of Jesus, I always notice his hands. Much of the time, the artist shows the hands of Jesus as soft and nearly effeminate. I believe the hands of this manly man were tough from his years in the carpenter's shop, on the fishing boats, and due to hundreds of miles of traveling.

Jesus was a man who believed in touching others. As you read the gospels, many of Jesus' miracles were done through touching the afflicted person. Jesus, as God's Son, only had to speak for healing to occur. However, it is worth noting how he usually took it a step further to include the needed human touch for people who had often been treated as outcasts by others.

Jesus touched others- the sick untouchable leper, the sinful woman avoided by others in her village, the eyes of a dirty blind beggar, an arm around the shoulder of a hated Samaritan- All were the recipients of the touch of the Master's hand.

In John 11, we encounter another gift of the Savior. As Jesus arrived in Bethany, he came to the home of his three special friends, a man named Lazarus, who lived with his two sisters, Mary and Martha. Lazarus became seriously ill and the sisters frantically sent for Jesus to come to Bethany. However, in a move that has mystified scholars to this day, Jesus delayed coming to his friend's rescue. In fact Jesus did not arrive until Lazarus had been dead for three days.

Jesus encountered a heart-wrenching scene of grief, tears, and sorrow as he came into the town of Bethany. In New Testament times, the Jewish communities in Israel spent days mourning and grieving at the home and graveside of the deceased. When Jesus neared Bethany, Martha ran to him and mildly chastised him (John 11:21) for not coming to the aid of his friend. Later, Mary also left the house and ran to meet Jesus. Her comment was basically the same, "Lord, if you had been here, my brother would not have died."

Then an amazing thing happened- Jesus, accompanied by the two sisters and the group of mourners, went to the grave of Lazarus. As Jesus looked around at the grieving and weeping family and friends, John 11:35 simply states, "Jesus wept."

We've often overlooked this shortest verse in the Bible. I laugh as I recall it was always the favorite verse of boys who had to learn a scripture verse for church.

"Norman, tell us your verse?" "John 11:35- "Jesus wept."

However, this simple two-word verse could be the subject of dozens of sermons. "Jesus wept." It confronts us with the fact that the fully divine Jesus had *fully* human emotions. I once heard this verse interpreted in this way:

Many people wonder as to why Jesus wept. His tears were not for Lazarus. Jesus knew that in a matter of minutes, Lazarus was going to come bursting out of that grave alive. Instead, his tears were the result of seeing the open, raw grief of those whom he loved. His weeping contained tears of compassion, tears of both sympathy and empathy for Mary, Martha, and for the crowd of mourning friends standing around the grave. His weeping was a wonderful gift, given from the heart of Jesus, the King of Kings, as He shared this "gift of tears" with them.

I firmly believe that Jesus still shares with us this gift of his compassion and tears. As I Peter 5:7 states, "Casting all of your cares on Him, because he cares for you."

As I shared earlier in this book, one of my opportunities for ministry is assisting families at our cemetery. In addition, I am often asked to share a word at funerals. I am not an ordained minister, but I'm always honored to warmly share about a loved one and remind those present about God's comfort and love.

My dad likes to pick at me and say, "Curt, no one in Dry Creek can be buried without you or Don Barrett helping send them off." Seriously though, it is a way I can help families and it even serves as part of the grieving process for me.

At most funeral services throughout the South, the ministers presiding at funeral services will stand beside the open casket as those present slowly file by to "pay their respects" one last time. This is a time beyond adequate description as you silently witness the deep emotion of watching lifetime friends and neighbors come by for one last goodbye.

For some reason at funerals I am able to keep my emotions in check as I stand in the pulpit and share. In fact, I was able to speak at two of my grandparent's services and make it through all right.

But standing beside an open casket as the weeping family begins passing by just rips my heart out. All of the friends and others have passed by and left the room. Only the family remains.

Slowly, one by one, or in small groups, they come for one last viewing. It is hard to describe the grief of a weeping granddaughter leaning down into the casket, laying her head on the chest of a grandfather whom she will miss for the remainder of her life- Or the face of an elderly husband, supported on each side by a son, as he looks one final time into the face of his true love of over sixty years. He stands there a long time just looking into the face of this woman with whom he has shared the ups and downs of a lifetime. Time seems to stop as he stands there. No one tries to rush him because this is a sacred time.

At this moment I always think of a story shared with me by Wayne Green, one of our community's best storytellers. He related that once at a funeral in Reeves, an old faithful husband stood at the coffin of his dear wife. As he stood there wordlessly, a younger nephew went up to him, and as he put his arm around his shoulder said, "Don't worry, Uncle Bud, it won't be long before you'll be joining her."

Wayne said he thought how cruel this statement was, until he realized how comforting it was to the old gentleman.

These scenes, and many others like it, always cause me to weep. I'm not talking about misty eyes, but just plain old crying. I can't help it, because as I see the raw and fresh sorrow of this family, the emotion is so deep that only tears can express it. At one time I was embarrassed by these tears. However, I've learned in my journey that the best gift I can give this family is my tears. By simply standing with them and weeping, I am able to give something more valuable than any words I have spoken.

The story is told of two young boys who were sitting on the steps of an apartment, both of them crying their eyes out. One of the boys had his arm around the shoulder of the other as they both wept. A passing adult stopped, and out of concern asked, "Hey guys, what are you crying about?"

One of the boys answered through his tears as to how he'd lost his dog. The second boy said, "Well, I was just walking by and I saw him crying, so I sat down and cried with him."

We smile at a story like that. Nevertheless, there is a great truth to it. One of our responsibilities is to sit and cry with those who are weeping. We should be looking for ways to minister and encourage each other. All of us are strugglers on this road of life. None of us have it all figured out. We need to simply be there for our fellow strugglers and put a compassionate arm around their shoulder.

Men, others are out there hurting and they need your physical presence, the comforting touch of your hand, a caring hug, and your gift of the tears of compassion.

"Keep 'er in Low Gear" on a Dead End Road

It seems like many of my stories revolve around our cemetery. I hope this doesn't seem morbid to my readers. As an emotional writer, I write of things of the heart and soul. Readers of my first book, Stories *from the Creekbank*, commented as to how they laughed, cried, and rejoiced as they read the book. One lady even said that we should supply Kleenexes with the book. I guess that is a compliment but I'm not quite sure exactly how she meant that.

I'm a writer and storyteller of the heart. I write about situations or people that touch us deep down in our soul. And I know of no other way that uncovers the raw nerves of our soul as does facing death.

But many times, the emotion I've seen, even at this sad time of death, one some of the funniest moments I've ever experienced. It may seem like strange bedfellows for humor and sorrow to travel together, but it has been my experience they do. This following story is built around one such event.

If you want to visit Dry Creek Cemetery you exit off Louisiana Highway 113 onto Morrow Bridge Road. After less than a mile on this side road, you will turn south onto the cemetery road. It winds through a series of curves as it passes several houses and ends at the wrought iron cemetery gate.

Frank Miller was one of my mentors who trained me for working at the cemetery. He taught me the art of dealing with families on selecting their burial sites. During this tender time, he showed the example of how to support and help those in grief. Through this ministry of love, I learned that there is not much we can say to comfort a grieving heart. However our presence, prayers, and hugs are remembered forever.

Mr. Frank came from a long line of Dry Creek pioneers. From his birth in Dry Creek in 1910 until his death in 1996, he saw most of the Twentieth Century. The following story occurred when he was about eighty years old.

I guess one of the reasons I best loved Mr. Frank was because of his great love for our community. He deeply loved Dry Creek throughout his life. He served as the unofficial historian of our area.

Mr. Frank was a master storyteller. His voice, inflection, mannerisms, and timing made everything he told memorable. Whether it was telling of sitting as a boy at the knee of gray-bearded Confederate veterans as they relived Shiloh or Vicksburg, or the growth of our community after the Depression, he had a remarkable memory and a gift for sharing his memories in a humorous and entertaining way. Many times as he told a story, he'd get so tickled before the punch line, that he'd begin laughing and could hardly finish the story.

Some of my most memorable times with Mr. Frank Miller would be when we would meet at the cemetery for a burial. He would carefully make sure everything was in order. When the service was over and the crowd dispersed, he would sidle up to me and say, "It was sure done the right way."

He had such a respect for the dignity of the final act of laying a body to rest. Often he referred to it as "The Dry Creek Way." By this he meant doing things in a dignified manner, mixed with kindness and compassion.

About twelve years ago, I helped him on a burial of the person whose body had been cremated. This method of burial, was very different from the usual process of a placing an embalmed body in a casket. Cremation was not considered "The Dry Creek Way," especially to Mr. Frank and his generation.

I'll always remember my wife's grandmother, Rita Terry, upon learning a relative wanted to be cremated, replying humorously, yet tartly, "Well, you've always tried to live as close to Hell as you could, so I guess that's what you ought to do."

And Grandma Terry's and Mr. Frank's feelings on cremation pretty well reflected the way their generation thought.

Recently I was in Atlanta, Georgia. As always, I enjoy reading a big city newspaper. After reading papers like the

Atlanta Constitution, fighting big city traffic, and hearing sirens all night long, I'm always ready to return home to the country. As I scanned the Atlanta paper, I came across the Obituaries Page. Hundreds of names were listed with short notices of their life, survivors, and burial services. It caught my attention that about ninety-percent of the dead had been cremated. I know this is due to crowded space and the expense of cemetery plots in big cities. However, I knew this would never have met Mr. Frank Miller's approval because it wasn't **the** Dry Creek Way.

I thought about how many of these deceased Atlantans would have funerals with small crowds and little notice by others as traffic speeds by the funeral procession.

In rural Louisiana, small communities stop when a funeral service takes place. Even the most humble citizen receives a respectful sendoff. As the hearse and procession pass down the highway, people pull off to the side of the road and stop to show their respect. I once remember being in a procession when a burly log truck driver stood outside of his cab, respectfully standing with his cap in his hand.

I recall Dry Creek native, Mr. Clyde Hanchey. Even when he was old and feeble, he continued to attend every funeral in our part of Beauregard Parish. Mr. Clyde had a deep respect for, and an enjoyment of people. He felt his personal attendance was honoring to the deceased and a comfort to the family. Moreover, this wise and caring man was right.

That is the Dry Creek Way. Although our friends in Atlanta and other big cities might consider us backward, I'd say the respect shown for people, both dead and alive, in our rural areas is much better than what is found in urban areas. In a small community like ours, you see and know the people you see daily, or pass on the road. It's hard to be rude to a driver who pulls out in front of you, when you know you'll sit by them later this week at a tee-ball game.

The story I'm about to relate happened just a few years before Mr. Frank Miller died. Our local police jury workers (these are the crews who keep our rural roads in good shape) decided to help direct travelers with a sign at the turnoff where the cemetery road veers right. They put up a green sign signifying the turn to the cemetery.

However, they also put up a second sign. I didn't even notice it until it was brought to my attention by Mr. Frank. One day while I was at work, he came in to see me. He was visibly upset and I could tell something had happened he was not pleased with. Immediately, he began telling me about a yellow diamond-shaped sign past the turnoff to the cemetery. Mr. Frank, with grave seriousness (excuse the pun) said, "Have you seen that sign on the cemetery road? They've put up a road sign that says, "DEAD END."

Sometimes I'm kind of slow, and it took me a while to grasp what he said. To be honest I thought he was joking. It took everything I had not to burst out laughing. When I saw how serious he was, I stifled my laughter.

Mr. Frank continued, "Curt, that is a lack of respect for our cemetery!" It should not say "dead end" on the road to our cemetery! Why, people will be making fun of it and our cemetery." I thought to myself , "I know a person who is making fun about it right now, at least on the inside, and it's me!"

Finally Mr. Frank stated, "We need to get the Board together and do something about this." With that he left out, not even touching his cup of coffee. As soon as it was safe, I drove to the cemetery road to see it for myself and there it was, bigger than Dallas- A big yellow sign, meant to get your attention. On it were black letters stating: DEAD END.

As much as I respected Mr. Frank I had to tell this story to his grandson, Ricky Gallien, a very special friend of mine. We both had a good time as we enjoyed the irony of this story.

A few weeks later Mr. Frank came to see me again. I could tell from his demeanor that he felt much better than on our last visit. Quickly he came to the point, "Curt, I've been thinking. We could get the police jury to change that sign to something less offensive. I've done some studying and I've come up with what I think is a good solution. The French word for dead end is 'CUL DE SAC'. We could replace the current sign with one reading 'CUL DE SAC."

Once again, I attempted to master the difficult balancing act of being sober-faced on the outside and bursting out laughing on the inside. I must have done all right because he continued with his plan, oblivious to my looking away not to break out laughing.

When he had finished, I waited a respectful while and said, "Mr. Frank, I can tell you've put a lot of thought into this. My only concern is that most people in Dry Creek have no idea what a 'cul de sac' is."

He replied, "Yes that is true, but it would sure be better than that dead end sign."

A few months later I noticed the Dead End sign was gone. I wanted to ask Mr. Frank if he knew who removed it, but I didn't have the nerve. In my mind I could see this eighty-five-year old man, in the darkness of night, pulling the sign up, and dumping it in Mill Bayou on his way home.

I never heard Mr. Frank mention the dead end sign again. Not too long after the sign disappeared, Mr. Frank died from a stroke. After his funeral service, as we drove down the cemetery road in the long line of vehicles, I smiled as we passed the spot where the dead end sign had been. Tears came to my eyes, as I thought about how much I would miss my special friend. However, at the same time, I felt warm inside as I cherished all of the stories, memories, advice, and mentoring given me by this memorable man.

As we went into the cemetery and carried his body to its final resting spot, I once again understood why Mr. Frank Miller loved this cemetery so much. All around his burial spot were the graves of five of his brothers, his parents, and his grandparents. As we placed his casket over the open grave, I was standing by the marker of his beloved wife of fifty-nine years, Mrs. Versie. Inscribed on the tombstone of this kind and loving woman, as her epitaph, was her favorite saying, "Well, bless your sweet little heart."

In my mind I saw them together again- slowly driving down the highway in their green car, in no hurry and with no more illnesses, cares, or death to face. God spoke reminding me in my heart, that death is not really "a dead end." Yes, it is the end of our finite existence in this perishable body. But eternal life, which is true life, continues on when our tired old body is laid to rest.

As I often do when standing here at a graveside, I recall the words of Jesus in John 11, "I am the resurrection and the life. He who believes in me will live again. I am the resurrection and the life, he who believes in me shall never die. Do you believe this?"

Over the next few months, I drive to the cemetery from time to time. My trips are to check for armadillos getting in under the fence or the cleanliness of the rest rooms. I smile each time as I pass the cemetery turnoff. I nearly expect to see a bright yellow sign reading: CUL DE SAC.

One day as I walk through the cemetery to the west of the tall cedar tree, I spot Mr. Frank and Mrs. Versie's tombstone. I go over and read the words on his marker. It states, "Keep 'er in low gear." I laugh aloud at this fitting epitaph. His grandchildren told me this was always his parting shot as they left after a visit. "All right keep 'er in low gear . . . and be careful."

As I walk away it reverberates in my brain, "Keep 'Er in low gear." And the thought hits me, I was glad I'd traveled "The Dry Creek Way," even if there was a dead end sign on the road leading to it.

A Prayer Answered by a Shaggy Dog

Many times the way God answers prayer is so creative that if we aren't careful, we will miss the answer and shrug it off to luck or coincidence. One of the major goals of our lives should be constantly looking and being sensitive to how God is always at work around us. I love the words of Jesus in John 5:17, "Jesus said to them, 'My Father is always at work, and I too, am working.'"

Sometimes we look at people, challenges, and situations and wonder where God is. But according to the words of Jesus, the Son of God, His Father is always at work, and He seems to work best in the midst of impossible situations and hard hearts.

First of all, our job is to recognize where, and how He is working and get involved there. Most of us are familiar with the words of author Henry Blackaby in *Experiencing God*, "Find where God is working and get involved in it."

We must remember how God does answer prayer in his own way... and His own time. God's timing is often different from ours, and that is where we often sidetracked.

The following story from last summer clearly reveals how creative God is as He meets our needs. In my mind I know this is a story of how God answered a prayer and the answer came in the form of a shaggy, smelly, runaway dog.

Eric Johnson is our summer staff leader at Dry Creek Baptist Camp. Eric, a recent graduate of Louisiana Technical University, is one of the most compassionate and gifted young leaders I've ever worked with. His unique blend of commitment to God, humble spirit, a fun loving sense of humor, and prayerfulness all combine to make him a man God is using. This story is about Eric, a shaggy dog, and a friend named Chris.

On the morning of our first youth camp, I arrived early. The first day of camp is a hectic time and I wanted to ensure everything was ready. As I stepped out of my truck at the office, I was greeted by the shaggiest, nastiest, and most downtrodden looking dog I'd ever seen.

He was a stubby and shaggy-haired dog with the pug-nosed face of a Pekinese. You could not see his eyes because the long hair hung down in his face. His gray coat was matted and stringy. Much of this coat, especially the long hair on his paws and his stomach hung down to the ground, coated with mud. To top it off, he smelled terrible. You've heard the saying, "He smelled like a wet dog." In this dog's case it was very true. He had a bad odor that hit you even before you got very close.

Our camp's location, at the intersection of Dry Creek's only two highways, and our proximity to Foreman's Meat Market, make us a haven for stray dogs. These dogs also instinctively know that a camp of three hundred preteen campers is a beggar's feast. Just standing by the exit door of the Dining Hall usually means a fine meal of leftovers handed out by campers.

Normally, stray dogs at camp must be quickly moved or given away. We cannot take the chance of a strange dog biting one of our campers. My first reaction to this sorry looking mutt was to put him in the back of my truck and haul him far enough away where he couldn't find his way back.

However, I bent down and moved his long hair from his eyes. He had those intelligent laughing eyes that fine dogs have. I spoke out loud, "I'd sure like for you to tell me your story, buddy. I bet it'd be an interesting tale of where you've been and how you got here."

There was no doubt this dog was a stray. I'd never seen a more neglected-looking dog. However, I also noticed that, oddly, he was not skinny looking from malnutrition as you see with most stray dogs.

Taking a second look at him, I said, "Little fellow, it looks like you've been down on your luck and out on the road for a while." His appearance reminded me of the forlorn threadbare dress of homeless people I've seen in big cities.

But this second glance revealed something else. Beneath all of the grime and matted hair, there was a quiet dignity about this male dog. His bushy tail stood erect and wagged as I spoke to him. I recalled the story of "The Prince and the Pauper" where the young prince was dressed in the rags of a beggar boy. I wondered if under this matted coat, a fine dog might exist

Those dark eyes looked happily at me. The whole time I was stroking his head, his small tongue constantly licked his lips as if he expected a snack from me. I could nearly swear there was a humanlike smile on his face.

Then weakness hit me. I really love dogs and the older I get, the more pitiful I am at what I'll do to take care of one. So I said, "We're going to keep you and make you our honorary camp dog for the week. For the time being, we'll name you "Hippie."

He wagged his tail and followed me. After a short walk, I looked around and he had quietly disappeared. He had quickly exposed the defining trait of his personality- "I love you, but you don't own me. I've been a vagabond dog for a long time, so don't fence me in."

Later that day as campers arrived, many of the youth noticed Hippie. He was hard to miss with that shaggy coat, frisky walk, and happy smile. Out in front of the Dining Hall, he lay on the sidewalk and tucked his head in under his front paws. In this position with his long shaggy coat, he looked just like an old-worn out dust mop. Some of the kids began calling him, "Moppy."

As camp started I knew we had to clean this little fellow up. This is when Eric Johnson entered this dog's life and a prayer was answered. Eric shares a common trait with me- He also has a terrible weakness for dogs. So, Eric fell in love with him too. As we discussed what to do to make this new camp dog presentable, I thought about my new friend Chris.

I had met Chris earlier in the summer. He was new to our community. My pastor, Don Hunt had visited him and shared with me about him. Chris had come to live with his mother as he suffered through the final stages of AIDS. I knew Chris' mother, Goldie, from my years as a school administrator. We had got to know each other well when she would come see me anytime one of her younger boys got in trouble. She loved a good fight and liked to get right up in my face. In spite of this, I really liked her and found that when she cooled off, she was easy to work with.

I didn't even know Goldie had an older son. As I heard about Chris' plight, I heard the sweet, but powerful voice of Jesus saying, "Go minister to him." Now, this was not something I was really excited about, but I knew I needed to go see him.

I arrived and knocked hesitantly on the trailer door. Deep down inside I hoped no one would answer. But the door opened and there was a gaunt and pale man who looked to be in his early thirties. Beside him a small Chihuahua barked fiercely.

Chris looked at me with as much hesitation as I had in knocking on the door. His look said, "I'm avoiding people because they avoid me." After what seemed a long time, he finally invited me inside the dark trailer. All of the window shades were drawn and the room had a feeling of depression to it. I sat down on the couch and we tried to visit and make small talk. There was very little we had in common, so it was hard to find a conversation opener. I could sense he was hesitant to open himself up and our visit was awkward.

After a while, I could tell he was beginning to enjoy having company. I wondered if anyone ever visited him other than his mother. I already knew the rest of his family would have nothing to do with him.

I knew Chris' homosexual lifestyle had led to this sad place in his life. Nevertheless, I also knew condemnation was not what he needed today. I just heard the voice of Jesus saying, "Minister to him in My name." This was really not an assignment I had signed up for, but I now knew what my marching orders were.

After visiting a while, I rose to leave. I just could just feel God leading me to simply touch Chris on the shoulder and pray with him. I knew it was God's way of saying through me, "I care about you." Due to the way AIDS patients are shunned, a physical touch or kind word is a rare and great gift.

Driving home, I had one of those brief encounters when I knew God spoke to me way down deep in my soul and deep in my heart where His voice cannot be ignored or misunderstood. It was simple, clear, and powerful all at the same time, "Don't let him die alone. Do not let him die alone."

On my next visit later that week, Chris seemed more relaxed and so did I. As I sat down on the couch, I was faced with one of those moments that will cement or destroy a new friendship. Chris said, "Mr. Iles, would you like a glass of tea?" Briefly I hesitated. In these several seconds, which seemed much longer, a thousand thoughts rushed through my brain. Most of them had to do with an AIDS patient handling a glass, ice, and tea that I would later hold to my lips.

Before I knew it, "Why, sure I'd like a glass" came right out of my mouth. Chris fixed me a large glass of iced tea with a big slice of lemon. It was really good tea and I commented on its taste. I knew the important thing was that I'd passed one more test of showing Chris I was going to be his friend.

On subsequent visits Chris began to share about his spiritual life. There was no doubt he had lived a sinful, sad, and painful life. But he also shared that he knew he had received forgiveness from God. He strongly told me that Jesus is the Son of God and the only way into Heaven. A look of peace was on his face as he said, "I know Jesus will be waiting to welcome me in to Heaven soon."

All I could think about was the wonderful story of the thief on the cross. This criminal, who had also lived a painful life of sin, did at least one thing right in his life- He turned to Jesus as he was dying and asked the Son of God in one simple sentence of great faith, "Jesus remember me when you come into your kingdom."

And Jesus' succinct but eternal reply was, "Today, you will be with me in paradise."

After several weeks of visiting with Chris, I finally discovered something we could talk about in common: He loved dogs. In fact, most of his working life in south Florida was spent as a dog groomer. All I had to do is ask him a dog-related question, and he would relate story after story of dealing with dogs of all sizes and dispositions, and the often-eccentric behavior of their human owners.

So weeks later, when the stray dog arrived, Chris came to my mind. Eric Johnson stood beside me as we discussed the need for a dog haircut.

By now, our dog had acquired several names. Our teenage staffers called him "Lenny" after longhaired singer Lenny Kravitz. Our office staff named him "Happy," which described his personality. So I turned to Eric and asked, "Eric, did you know my friend Chris is a dog groomer?"

Eric said, "Really?" and then added, "Great, I'll call him and see if he wants to take on the biggest challenge of his life by shearing Happy."

The next day, Eric picked up Chris to bring him to the camp to groom Happy. First of all, they had trouble finding the shaggy little dog. Being a very independent dog, he never stayed in one area of the camp very long. He could usually be found wolfing down food brought to him by campers. He was definitely enjoying a good time as the adopted camp dog and had found what country people call, "A bird nest on the ground." That is a rural term for someone being in an easy and good situation.

Finally, Eric and Chris found him hiding under the porch at the First Aid building. Being a longhaired dog in the Louisiana summer heat is not very comfortable, so he had found a shady spot to stretch out in.

When Chris saw him, he excitedly exclaimed, "Why, that dog is a Lhasa Apso. This is a rare breed of dog that originated in Tibet. In ancient Asia, it was against the law for anyone but royalty to own a Lhasa Apso. They were kept in palaces as watchdogs, because of their keen sense of hearing." Having heard him bark, I could understand why he'd be a good watchdog because of his urgent and shrill bark which sounded much louder than the size he was.

As Happy sauntered up to Chris, Eric, and I, I looked at his mangy appearance and told him, "Buddy, if you're a kingly dog, you've lost your kingdom and fallen on pretty hard times." But even as I said this, I once again noticed the erect and dignified way in which he carried himself-evidently there was a certain bit of royalty in this mangy mutt that went back to his proud ancient royal ancestors.

Chris had bought electric clippers at Wal-Mart and had an old pair of scissors. I go on about my business as Eric and Chris take on the chore of making a decent looking dog out of Happy.

Several hours later, I returned to see the three of them right where I'd left them. Eric and Chris were covered with dog hair and both were soaking wet with sweat. Happy was about half sheared. I looked at Chris' pale face and could see that he was totally worn out.

Eric explained that all three of them have had enough for the day. They'll finish tomorrow with round two. Happy now had a spring to his step, but he was a long way from being neatly groomed. He grinned at me as if this half haircut suited him just fine.

Later that evening Eric came to talk with me. His voice was emotional as he relates the following, "Bro. Curt, last Friday I spent the whole day in prayer. God really spoke to me about having more compassion in my life. I asked him to give me an opportunity to show the compassion of Jesus to someone who was not easy to love. I believe He answered my prayer in a way I didn't expect.-He answered it with a shaggy stray dog."

Eric continued, "Because of this dog, I got the opportunity to meet Chris. It gave me the chance to minister to someone that most people would not be willing to do. I just felt the spirit of Jesus telling me to be his friend and that little dog was the common ground I needed to minister to Chris. My prayer for compassion was answered by God through this dog."

Eric's words touched me and once again I turned to the amazing Jesus, the Son of God, and silently thanked Him for the creative and surprising way He works. I was also amazed by the spiritual sensitivity in Eric, who is half my age. Once again, I realized that young people are often our best teachers.

The next day Eric brought Chris to camp to continue grooming "Happy." Today was my turn to hold the dog while Chris sheared. I quickly discovered why Eric was so sweaty the day before. Happy didn't like being sheared, especially under his belly and between his legs. He squirmed and fought my grip on him. He was amazingly strong for a small dog. When the clippers nicked him, he would snap toward Chris's hand. He wanted to bite, but had too sweet a disposition to actually do it. I was amazed at how quick Chris was in avoiding the teeth. He told Happy, "Fellow, you'll have to be a lot quicker than that to get me. I've been doing this a long time."

Over the next hour and a half, I watched an artist at work. Chris carefully trimmed and groomed this dog until he had a completely new look- a look of neatness which he hadn't previously had. Then I looked at Chris. It alarmed me at how pale and tired he looked. I knew he had pushed his weak body to the point of exhaustion. However, even this pale look did not hide the look of satisfaction on Chris' face. He had just made a positive difference using the talent he possessed. I wondered how long it had been since he had truly felt useful and appreciated.

Then I looked at Happy, now licking his sheared rear foot, and said silently, "Boy, you sure needed a haircut. But, you didn't need Chris' help near as much as he needed yours."

I drove Chris home with Happy riding in the bed of the truck. Looking at Chris' tired and haggard look, I knew he would pay for this exertion over the next few days. However, I knew it was worth it for Chris to feel useful and alive again. As he got out of my truck, his final words were, "Thanks for letting me help. I really enjoyed it. I believe I may start grooming dogs again."

As I drove home, I looked back at Happy in the back of the truck. He had his paws up on the side of the bed as the wind whipped his coat. There was a look of great satisfaction on his face and I once again wished I could read his mind.

And I thanked God for how he answers prayer, this time in the form of a stray dog in need of a haircut. Then I also thanked Him for how He cleans us up- not with soap, water, and flea shampoo, but through his complete, total, and free forgiveness- all available through the fully paid "It is finished" death of His son Jesus.

Later down the road...

It was six months later on a cool January day when we buried Chris. One of his last requests before dying was to have his memorial service at the camp. His comment was, "The camp is where I felt the most love and acceptance of my entire life."

A good crowd came to the service. It was so comforting to know Chris did not die alone, but was surrounded by love when he died and now as we shared sweet remembrances of his friendship. Best of all, it was a great opportunity to share about God's unconditional love through Jesus.

As the service ended and we prepared to go to the cemetery, I carried Chris' ashes, at the request of his mother, Goldie. As I walked to my truck, there stood Happy the dog. He had faithfully sat outside the Tabernacle during the service as if he knew what was going on.

At my invitation, he quickly hopped up in the truck. Arriving at the cemetery, I handed Chris' ashes to his mother for our walk across the grounds to Chris's gravesite.

Happy trotted along beside us. As Chris' family and friends gathered around the grave site and we had a time of closing prayer, Happy respectfully sat right beside Chris's grave- A shaggy dog who answered a prayer.

Sister Reddie

There are many stories I could tell about one of Dry Creek's oldest characters. I'll share just one story and you'll better understand why we love her so.

To fully enjoy this story, you must have a picture of this lady in your mind. First of all, let's get her name right. She spells it "Reddie" but to everyone in our community she is known as "Reedie." Additionally, most folks refer to her as "Sister Reddie." This in respect for her long service to God.

At the time of this writing, Mrs. Reddie is eighty-eight years old. She lives alone, still drives, and lives a full and active life. She is an inspiring role model for how an older person can just keep on going and not give up or "retire" from life.

Only last week she came to the camp office looking for a computer catalog to order some supplies. When I asked her if she uses the internet, she replied, "Yes, I sure do. I use it all of the time."

My first childhood memory of Mrs. Reddie is still indelibly pressed into my mind. She was at a church singing and playing a tambourine. Her rhythm and passion in playing it caught my attention. She was really working the tambourine over, and I couldn't take my eyes off her, and I've been fascinated with her ever since.

She's a lady who loves projects. Her latest project is writing and publishing books. She has written and published two books on the history of our local Pentecostal churches. I've read both of them and they are very well written and informative.

Mrs. Reddie is a small and short lady with a big and caring heart. Her short stature is set off by her hairstyle. Her hair is piled up high on her head in what is called a "beehive hairdo." Though her size is small, she fits the description of what we often call being "larger than life." In everything she does, she does it with all of her heart. I've never known her to do anything half-way. This following story is proof of this woman's determination and grit.

This story took place when she was "only" seventy-six years old. In June of that year, we had one of the worst floods ever to occur in our area. A creeping tropical storm settled over the northern Gulf and pumped a week's worth of steady rain into our area. By the end of the week, it had rained over fifteen inches. Most of the local creeks and rivers were flooded, resulting in many roads being closed.

As usual, nearby Bundick Lake flooded and swept into many fishing cabins and homes. Six miles south of the lake, Bundick Creek crosses Highway 113. This bridge crossing is called "Three Bridges" by our local folks. When the lake floods, the downstream creek, which drains the lake, flows out of its banks and spreads out over the nearby swamps. The highway acts as a levee and all of the rushing creek water backs up and then surges across the highway for a distance of sometimes up to a quarter mile. During this particular flood, traffic could not pass through on the highway for over three days.

One of the things that occur in a flood situation is that people leaving Dry Creek heading north cannot go past the flooded area on Highway 113. They are forced to make a long detour of up to forty-five miles. Because of this, people's frustration with the flooded road will often make them attempt to ford the waters, which is not very wise.

During this flood in 1989, the rain finally slackened and the muddy creek water slowly began to recede. A few big trucks and vehicles bravely forded the flooded area on the highway. As I watched these vehicles struggle through the floodwaters, I shook my head in amazement, recalling instances when cars had been washed off the road at that very spot.

One of my unofficial duties is being one of Dry Creek's flood inspectors. Each day during the flood, I would go down to Three Bridges and check the level on several marked stakes I'd driven in the ground alongside the flooded roadside ditch.

When I went down on Thursday afternoon to check the water level, I saw a startling sight where the creek water was still deep and dangerous as it rushed over the highway. There perched precariously on the edge of the roadway, right at the edge of a deep ditch, was a truck.

The floodwaters rushed around the red truck at a depth over the top of the tires. It was obvious that the rapid current had washed this truck off the road. The extreme angle of the truck, right where the shoulder dropped sharply to the ditch, made it appear as if any second, the truck would be washed off into the deep water.

A small crowd had gathered at each end of the flooded roadway to watch this drama unfold. I was standing there with my neighbor, Greg Spears. I told Greg, "That sure looks like Mrs. Reddie Harper's red GMC truck."

The water was about knee deep and unbelievably swift. As Greg and I waded out the strong current pulled us toward the deep east ditch. Every step took great effort. The thought of what would happen if we fell down stayed in my mind.

There ahead of us, balanced on the shoulder's edge, was the red truck. As we got closer, you could see the truck periodically shaking in the current. At any second I expected it to topple over. Nearing the truck, I could see a head not much above the top of the steering wheel. There was no mistaking the profile of Mrs. Reddie Harper's head and hair behind the steering wheel.

A group of men on the other side of the flooded highway had waded out to the truck first. As Greg and I waded up, they were imploring Mrs. Reddie, to get out of the truck and let them carry her to higher ground. However, no manner of begging could budge her.

The sight of this group of country men, standing in knee deep water futilely pleading begging this older woman to let them carry her out would have been laughable, if the situation hadn't been so serious. To each plea, her reply was steadfast and calm, "I'm not going anywhere. The Lord will take care of me right here in my truck."

One of the men said, "But, Mrs. Reddie, that truck could flip over any second into the deep ditch. Let us help you out."

We might as well been talking to the nearby trees swaying in the floodwater for all of the good it did. If you know Mrs. Reddie Harper, you know she is very headstrong. Well, let me go ahead and say it straightforward- she is just downright stubborn.

Anyway, her faith in the Lord was much stronger than persuasion by any would-be rescuers. Finally, a fellow in a truck with a winch drove into the water. Another man waded out and hooked the cable to the front bumper of her truck.

I'll never forget the breathless few seconds as the winch pulled the cable tight. The red truck lurched as if it was going to fall into the deep water. Any second we all expected the truck to wash over into the deep ditch.

But it never slipped in. Instead, with a shudder, the winch began to pull Mrs. Reddie and her truck to safety. I'll always remember the sight of her truck being pulled through the water. The first thing I noticed, as the truck came out of the water, was her front license plate which read, "Jesus Saves"

It became visible as she came out of the water. It was evident to everyone present that her license plate was true in more ways than one. Mrs. Reddie had great faith in the Lord … And who can argue with how God's protecting hand, and Mrs. Reddie Harper's faith, kept that truck upright during the flood of '89.

The Lord sits upon the flood;
Yes, the Lord sits as King forever.
Psalms 29:10

Lessons from the Birds

It's one of my favorite times of the year- early June. There are several reasons why I love the first two weeks of June. School is now out and kids are everywhere enjoying freedom from the confines of the classroom. I recall the chant of my childhood, "No more classes, no more books, no more teachers' dirty looks."

It's time for all of the rites of summer- It's now warm enough for swimming in the creek, and ripening blackberries are ready to be found in the thickets. In gardens, purple-hull peas are ready, and watermelon vines are beginning to run, a reminder that the end of June will yield those famous sweet Sugartown Watermelons.

Early June begins a special time for me- Summer camp! For the next twelve weeks we will have the joy of hosting thousands of campers of all ages.

Just like clockwork, this week of summer camp coincides with the first baby birds leaving their nests to fly. In the last two weeks I've seen several young birds hopping on the ground, old enough to leave the nest, but not quite ready to fly for any distance.

This is a dangerous time for any young bird. Due to their limited flying capacity these young birds are easy prey for cats and other predators.

Just last week our Labrador retriever, Ivory, trotted up to me in our yard. In her mouth was a squawking young mockingbird. She brought it right to me just as if we were in the duck blind and it was a mallard drake.

As I took the bird from Ivory's mouth, I was relieved to see that it was not injured other than being scared to death. I thought to myself how this bird would have a story to one day tell its grandchildren: "The infamous day when the large white monster captured it, when it was just a young fledgling."

I carefully placed the mockingbird on the limb of a nearby tree. It flapped its short wings but didn't move from its perch. I went out at dark and it was still perched right where I'd placed it. The next morning it was gone and I hopefully wished it was now flying somewhere high in the sky.

The very same week, I rescued a young blue jay from the ground at camp. It set up a howl when I caught it. With its long beak, it tried in vain to peck me. I carefully looked overhead to make sure I wasn't going to be dive-bombed by a mother jaybird, and then I placed it in some thick hedges for protection.

Then yesterday at the camp, two of our workers discovered a baby screech owl hopping on the ground. It was very aggressive and hard to handle. They placed it in a tree and it was gone the next morning.

I wasn't surprised to hear about the baby owl. Several weeks ago I had encountered an adult screech owl near this same spot. Walking out of my office after dark, I saw a shadowy figure fly by my ear. I knew it was probably an owl because of their nighttime habit of staying near outdoor lights and swooping down on small animals or insects.

I returned to the office and got my bird book. Going back outside I shined my light up into the nearby oak trees. There I spotted a small owl on an upper limb. Each time I shined the beam of light directly in his face, he would turn his head away from me. It is always amazing to watch an owl rotate his head in a nearly 180-degree turn.

I looked down at my bird book and found the pages on owls. Just as I was trying to tell from his size if he was a Barred Owl or Screech Owl, I felt a swoosh go by my ear. This owl was letting me know I was an unwelcome invader in his territory. When he dove on me the second time, I sought the refuge of my office before I got a claw mark across my bald head.

Peterson's *Field Guide to Birds*, the bible of all serious birdwatchers, clearly informed me that this new neighbor of mine was a screech owl. The screech owl is the smallest of American owls. It is only 7-10 inches tall, but its personality makes it think it is "ten feet tall and bulletproof." I smile as I read these words in the guidebook,

> *"This owl tends to be very aggressive when humans are in the area near their nest. They will often swoop down and harass passersby."*

I had first hand knowledge of that! Several nights later I saw two screech owls in the same tree. Carefully I walked away after watching them for a few minutes. Therefore, when our workers later found the baby owl which we, it didn't surprise me.

Then several days later, we found another baby owl on the ground. It might have been the same screech owl the boys had found earlier. We kept him for a couple of days and nicknamed him "Hootie." Then, I set him in a nearby tree near where we suspected the nest was. As I walked away, the owl was immediately attacked by a mockingbird. It was a fine fight with both of the birds about the same size. I told the mockingbird, (yes, I talk to birds. They are very good listeners.) "Buddy, you better whip 'Hootie' now, because in a few months he'll eat you for supper if he catches you in his talons!"

"Hootie", the screech owl

All around our community it is a special time for birds. Nests are full of chirping birds, all getting ready for their first flights.Each species of birds has their own personality. I believe that is why I love Purple Martins the most. These birds, members of the swallow family, are very social and prefer nesting in colonies in manmade boxes.

Before white explorers came to America, the Native Indians had already discovered the positive benefits of these birds. Martins only eat flying insects. Experts claim an adult martin can eat over 2000 mosquitoes per day. The Indians hung birdhouses made from dried gourds to attract these extremely social birds which seemed to prefer living near humans.

The early pioneers also adopted these birds, and it became very common to see Martin boxes of all sizes and shapes around their dwellings. Throughout America these birds are still loved and expectantly looked for each spring as they return from their winter homes.

To be adopted by Martins, the bird box must be out in the open and be raised to about twelve feet above the ground. Martins will only nest where there is adequate open space for their scooping, soaring, and acrobatic stunts, all performed while they catch insects. Moreover, their song is wonderful- It's hard to describe the song of this bird. I've heard it described in so many ways: "A bubbling sound going up and down." My favorite description is "A happy song." When I come outside on a spring morning and hear their playful singing, I feel happy knowing they are paying me the honor of spending part of the year with my family.

Even though I love these Martins, I am not immune from their wrath. As June arrives and the babies are hatching from the eggs, their parents become very protective. The young birds peek out of the nest holes, eagerly awaiting food from their parents.

As I approach the boxes, the babies quickly pull their heads back in and hide. I wonder how they have the instinct to hide from animals. As I stand there under the box, the attack begins. The adult Martins swoop and fly in the air. Their song is not as happy as usual, but it has more of an alarm to it. Then the bravest of the birds comes swooping down toward me. He doesn't try to actually hit me, but sweeps over my head as a warning to "back off!" Hearing the rush of its wings, I usually instinctively duck.

I can always recognize this particular brave male bird by an open space on one of its wings. There are several feathers missing in that area. I wonder what story is behind how this veteran was wounded in combat. Excuse my pun, but this bird probably won the "Purple Heart" for his wound in some earlier battle with their mortal enemies, Starlings and Sparrows.

The other less battle-hardened birds respectfully keep their distance. However, this one bird makes dive after dive. I really believe it's the highlight of his day to harass me or the dogs. He never seems to tire of his dive-bombing responsibilities.

As the days pass, the baby birds quickly grow bigger. It's is amazing how quick a baby bird can "feather up" and be ready to leave the box. One particular bird box hole at our house has three babies, sticking their heads out, awaiting their next meal. Observing them daily, I know it's just about time for them to venture out onto the box ledge and take their first flight. Sure enough, the next morning there are only two heads peeking out. By evening, one more is gone. The next day, the box is empty. Amid all of the swooping, diving, and constant chattering, I try to pick out these three new flyers, but I cannot distinguish them from the other Martins.

One day during that same week, I walk out into the yard. Under one of the bird boxes on the ground is a young Purple Martin, squawking loudly. This time, I beat Ivory to the bird, loudly instructing her to sit and stay. She looks at me as if to say, "I was born to retrieve birds for you and now you won't allow me to what I was born to do!"

I scoop the bird up. It is trembling and I can feel its heart pounding. As I stand there, I recall an old story:

Once a boy brought a caught bird to the home of the community's wisest man. Approaching the old sage, the boy cupped his hands around the small bird. 'Old man,' he said, 'You are supposedly so wise. So tell me, is this bird in my hand alive or dead?'

The boy, with a smirk on his face, waited for the answer. If the wise man answered, 'He is dead,' the boy would open his hands and let the bird fly off. If the answer was 'alive,' he would crush the bird in his hands. Either way he was sure he could outsmart the old man.

After a time of silence, the old man sagely replied, 'Only you know the answer to that, my son, only you know . . . and the answer lies in your hands.'"

With that thought in mind, I open my hands and toss the young Martin into the air. He struggles and flies a short distance before coming back to earth. Once again, I instruct Ivory to stay and not go after the bird. She whines with anticipation for the opportunity.

The grounded bird tries to escape me. Upon catching him, I once again toss him into the air. This time he flies a good distance before landing in our field among the high grass. I leave him there and hope the best for him.

In the next few days all of the young birds leave the nest. The sky is now filled with more Martins as the young birds join their parents in flight. They soar in the wind and it is easy to tell they are enjoying what they were born to do. Watching them, I understand why men in earlier times attempted to build machinery to fly. We humans are always subconsciously jealous when we see a soaring bird. The words of King David in Psalms 55:6 express this desire to fly, "Oh, that I had wings of a dove! I would fly away and be at rest."

Watching these young birds fly, the sad thought hits me as to how soon they will all be gone. One morning soon, probably in early July, I will walk outside to enjoy their singing and flying, only to find they are gone.

I think back to the previous February day when the first two Martin scouts arrived. It was a cold rainy day. I was surprised to see them this early and in such bad weather. This pair, a male and female, stayed throughout the day, huddled on the box ledge. Then, as abruptly as they had appeared, the birds disappeared. However, I knew they would eventually be back. Sure enough, within a week they were back with their entire colony of Purple Martins.

One of the reason I love Martins so much is because of my mom's dad, my Grandpa Sid Plott. I believe I inherited his love for these remarkable birds and their travels. We spent many precious hour talking about Martins and the other birds of our area.

Even now when the first Martin scout arrives, I always think of my Grandpa and his love and respect for Purple Martins. Each year when the first birds begin arriving at my boxes, I feel that same love and kinship. When you understand about this unique bird's migratory journey, I believe you will respect it also.

Purple Martins spend their winters in Brazil. There they nest in hollow trees and live among the great expanse of the Amazon jungle. Sometime after the first of the year, they begin preparing for their long flight north. When their instincts tell them the time is right, they begin flying in small groups northward. Ornithologists tell us they fly in small groups to avoid whole colonies being wiped out due to encountering storms over the Gulf.

Following their long journey across the Gulf of Mexico, they reach mainland North America. Upon arrival, they regroup into large flocks near large bodies of water. Here they replenish and rest after their exhausting flight. Their only food is flying insects, so the proximity to large areas of water, means plenty of food for everyone. Should they arrive in North America too early, or if there is a late cold spell, insects may not be present, and the Martins must return southward or starve. That is why their inner clock of leaving South America is so important. This is even more amazing when we realize their winter home in the area of the equator has no cold weather to push them out, such as we see with waterfowl.

Shortly after grouping up in these large colonies along the southern coast, the Martin scouts head back to the exact site of the previous year's nesting site, which is the place of birth for most of the colony. There is some difference of opinion concerning how the scouts travel to and from the nesting site. There is speculation they navigate to their homes by the position of the stars. However, their unerring travel, even in overcast weather, raises questions concerning that theory. It's enough to say that they have a unique inner instinct to hone in on their birthplace.

To my way of thinking, the marvelous instinct possessed by these birds is a clear indication of a Master Designer. I always think of God, the Great Creator, when these birds faithfully return to their summer boxes throughout the United States and southern Canada. As I shared earlier, the scouts are the first to actually return to their northern homes. After a thorough inspection of the boxes, they then disappear. Within a few days or weeks, the entire colony will return to their place of birth, led by the mature and experienced birds. During their journey across Brazil, the Gulf, and up through most areas of the eastern United States, some will fly a distance of eight thousand miles from their South American home to the box where they will raise their young.

Standing by my three boxes in June, I stand watching these Martins fly about and think about their upcoming journey of thousands of miles back to South America. In the next few weeks the sight of these larger groups both thrills and saddens me at the same time. I am glad how this year's crop of babies has been large. However, knowing how quiet it will be when they leave saddens me.

As the days of late June slip by, the Martins spend less and less time around the bird boxes. This morning I counted thirty-six sitting on a high line wire in my field. They are gathering in these large groups in preparation for their journey to their large roost areas closer to the Gulf, followed by their long flight south to Brazil.

Daily, the adult Martins are taking the young birds on longer flights to prepare them for the challenging journey they will take in the next few months. Knowing their habits, it is clear that very soon, I will walk outside one morning to find the noisy singing and acrobatic flying I love so much gone. It's always a sad day when the Martins leave in July, knowing I won't see them again until February. However, at the same time I'm happy to have enjoyed another year with these friends. I remind myself they are doing what they were born to do- leaving the nest to fly high and far. Even though I'd like to keep them year round, I would never deny them the freedom and adventure of their long journey across two continents and the Gulf of Mexico.

Pondering how quiet it will be when these birds are gone, I think about a conversation I had last night at the ballpark. DeDe and I were at a baseball game for our youngest son. Watching twelve-year-old Terry play first base, I thought to myself, "It's only yesterday he was playing T-ball and now he is ready to move up to the next level of the game he loves."

Mark Newsom is on the team we are playing against tonight. Mark was born one day after Terry in 1989. Both boys were born at Beauregard Memorial Hospital in DeRidder. Mark is the son of our special friends, Steve and Debbie Newsom.

Terry was one day old and we were preparing to take him home from the hospital, when Mark was born. He was premature and weighed slightly over three pounds. Mark was immediately moved to the hospital in Lake Charles. Because of his low birth weight, he was in extremely serious condition. Everyone prayed hard for Mark and his family.

Now, looking behind home plate, there is Mark Newsom, twelve years later. He stands there in his catcher's gear, with blonde hair poking out from below his helmet. His uniform is dirty and both knees have grass stains that Debbie will have the challenge of removing. Mark is tall and lanky, taller than most boys his age. He moves with the graceful stride of a gifted athlete. I'm thankfully amazed that this fine young man is the same tiny baby we prayed so fervently for twelve years ago.

Once again I hear the song of the Martins in my head as the young birds learn the joy of soaring and diving. Mark and Terry have sure grown up quickly. Before we turn around, they will be sending each other high school graduation invitations.

Following the game we visit with Steve and Debbie. When I inquire as to what their older son, Brent, is doing this summer, they inform us that he is currently in China doing short-term missions. He is officially there to teach American culture and English at a Chinese University, but his real purpose is to share the love of Jesus as he has opportunity. The Newsoms don't even know what town he is in and have no means of contact with him. They simply know he is somewhere in China for the next few months. I ask Debbie, "How can you sleep at night not being sure where your son is in a strange and hostile land?"

Her face shows a tremendous sense of peace as she replies, "God made it clear to me a long time ago that Brent was going to be in missions and probably live far away. So, I've had some time to get ready for this."

Then, I see the young Martins, silhouetted against the sky, making their first long journey across the ocean. Through both clear blue skies, and in the midst of storms, they fly on, guided by the stars and the instinctive internal compass God has placed within their tiny bodies.

Next, I recall an e-mail I just received from Kenya. It was from Troy Ketchum, one of our former counselors. His e-mail shared how he has traveled into the wilds of Western Kenya to minister to an unreached tribe. From his e-mail messages, it is clear God is stirring his heart and preparing Troy for a special part in missions also.

All over my open fields, the Martins swoop up and down, simply enjoying the thrill of soaring and gliding. Their parents carefully watch from a nearby electrical line.

Then my mind drifts to my own three boys. The older two, Clay and Clint, will both be serving as missionaries this summer. Clay will be in Canada and Clint will work in inner city ministry in Greenville, South Carolina. I joke with them as to how God may be calling them to go in the future as missionaries to Sugartown or Reeves (our neighboring villages to the north and south of Dry Creek.) But deep inside, I know there is a good chance my boys may one day be serving in far off lands. I think about the culture and location my grandchildren may grow up in.

Crossing the vast ocean through a strong wind mixed with fog and rain, the young Martins near complete exhaustion and seem ready to fall from the sky. However, one of the mature birds, a long-time veteran of this trip, flies nearer and silently wills the young birds to continue on. Then through a break in the clouds, the coast of South America looms below. They've made it- their first trip to their winter home.

Thinking of my boys and where they may be going, I'm reminded that the best, happiest, and safest place to be is in the center of God's will. This is all I can ask from God- for Him to lead my boys into this special place in His will, wherever that may be.

Finally, one last time before going inside, I watch all of the younger Martins gathering on the electrical line, ready for their big flight.

Just as I would never stop these birds from going where God, through instinct, has sent them, I know I would not stop my boys, nor any of the special young people I know and love, from their journey to find God's will for their lives.

It's nearly dark now and as I walk back to the house, I'm happy. I'm very happy knowing that at least for today, I've got my Martins, and my three sons, to be with and enjoy.

Purple Martin habitat information gleaned from the excellent book, *"What you should know about the Purple Martin."* J.L.Wade 1966 Griggsville, IL.

An Unbroken Circle of Music

One of life's greatest joys is gathering with friends and family to share together in something we all enjoy. It may be fishing, playing dominoes, or just eating a meal together. But anything we do with those we love multiplies the joy.

Therefore, on nights when we gather together with our friends to play music, it is always special. When a group of folks sit together to play music, it is a feeling which cannot adequately be described, but must be instead experienced.

My main influence in music has always been my dad. I know of no one who loves to sing more than him. I've never seen him fail to sing when asked, whether it is at church, a front porch singing, or a funeral.

When he sings it is very evident that he is singing from deep down in his heart. He sways and his deep bass voice resounds with emotion. It is hard to describe his singing, so authentic and basic; it just seems to come directly from his soul.

I also know from playing the drums behind him for most of my life that each time he sings a song, today's rendition will be slightly different from the hundreds of times I've heard him sing it. I never know when he is going to hold out a note or change the cadence. It's kind of like riding down the road on a dark night with one dim headlight. You know where you're going, but you aren't sure how or when you're going to get there.

My dad's repertoire at our Saturday night singings is what I would call "eclectic." Eclectic is simply a word that means a mixture of things on which you just can't quite pin a label. I always know that "Just a Closer Walk with Thee" will be followed by some ballad like "The Folsom Prison Blues" or "Springtime in Alaska."

Then just as quickly we'll shift back to "When the Roll is Called Up Yonder" or "Unclouded Day. "

As a boy, my family would sing as we traveled in our car. Both of my sisters were good singers and they would join in all of those Hank Williams classics or a lively version of "Old Dan Tucker." I didn't sing much because I was self-conscious about my singing voice.

Later, during my young teenage years of rebellion, I openly let them know I didn't care for those twangy country songs. I had my own style of music and preferred Creedence Clearwater Revival and The Allman Brothers over Loretta Lynn and Merle Haggard. I would stare out the window during those car singing sessions, feigning disinterest as they sang, but deep inside I was enjoying the songs I'd grown up on. Even now if my dad forgets a line on one of those old classics, I can pretty well lean over the drums and whisper the lines.

During my teen years, my love of rock music brought lot of humorous comments from my dad. Control of the car radio was a major battleground in my family. Once, when it was my turn and the radio was tuned into a rock station, Three Dog Night came on singing, "Eli's Coming." My dad put his hand on the radio and commented, "Someone open up that radio and let that man out. He's screaming like he's in pain." Even though I never wanted to, I couldn't help but burst out laughing at comments like that.

As I left home for college and began my own life, I found my own musical tastes changing. The disco age of the seventies turned my country heart completely off. Suddenly, some of Dad's kind of music appealed to me. Even more astonishing was the fact that he was learning to enjoy the Southern style of music I loved.

During this time of my life we didn't have as many singings, at least those I could attend. As the years rolled on, and I moved back to Dry Creek, we began to get together to sing more. There were a few constants from my boyhood, such as my dad's love of those old ballads and hymns. We'd gather together- my dad and Julian Campbell, the best "Chet Atkins" style guitarist in our area, would always take center stage at these singings. My brother-in-law Jody would join in on the piano or guitar, alongside my buddy Ed Shirley. Other musicians would come and go as we simply enjoyed sharing together in the bond of music.

When she wasn't playing the piano at the Catfish Hut, my Aunt Margie Nell would join us. Her piano style is so unique that I believe I could recognize it anywhere. One of my favorite things is to see my dad singing as his sister plays along. She is the only person I know who can play a song flawlessly, while carrying on a full conversation across the room.

One thing about Aunt Margie is how she'll pick out one of my favorites such as "Tara's Theme" from *Gone with the Wind*. As she launches into that song, she'll look at me across the top of the piano with such a smile of pure joy. She nods her head and winks at me and it is clear she is playing this song *just* for me. As we smile at each other, it's amazing to realize how love can be so clearly expressed through music.

Aunt Margie puts the same expression of joy and emotion into her playing as her brother, my dad, does in his singing. Their two unique styles and personalities combine to produce a style of music I've loved all of my life.

Margie Nell Walker

This story on Aunt Margie is one of my favorites:

When I was fifteen, my parents temporarily lost their minds and allowed me to ride a greyhound bus to Shreveport to see my favorite group, Creedence Clearwater Revival. I had learned to play the drums by listening to their songs over and over on scratchy albums. Daddy always said that if their drummer got sick, I could set in and play for them. I believe he meant it in jest, but I took it as a great compliment.

During the 1970's, Aunt Margie and Uncle Mark lived in Belcher, a small community north of Shreveport. When I arrived in Shreveport for the concert I called her to let her know I was in town. When she inquired as to why I was there, I told her I'd come to see Creedence Clearwater Revival.

You could hear the pleasure in her voice as she replied, "That's just wonderful how you've come this far to go to a revival." I didn't have the heart to correct her. Later, she told my mom how proud she was of my one hundred-sixty mile trip to attend a revival.

Aunt Margie's talent and joy in playing always seems to lift the other musicians to another level. It's amazing how a gifted musician can pull other ordinary musicians along in the wake of their talent.

At these Saturday night community singings, musicians with varying styles and tastes will join us. My friend, Vance Gill, who prefers more of a country style, joined us a few years ago, and added his unique singing style and guitar picking.

Then about two years ago, a strange thing began to happen at these get-togethers. Several teenage guitar players in our community began attending. Pretty soon there would be seven or eight guitar players there with a wide spectrum of styles that covered nearly every genre you could name.

One particular night specifically stands out in my mind. I'd called many of the younger players to come join us. After a mixture of older men and teenage boys had gotten tuned up, we begin playing. Usually during a singing, it takes thirty minutes or so for everyone to get comfortable. About this time, the door opened and in came an unknown teenager. In one hand he carried a beat up guitar case and in the other he lugged this huge amp.

What caught the older men's attention, and nearly stopped them in mid-song, was this boy's hair. His hair was dyed green. The closest description I could give would be that it was the same shade as Jim Carrey's hair in "The Grinch Who Stole Christmas."

I could see the look of wonderment on the faces of the older players who did not know "green hair." I saw a faint smile on the face of Rev. Frank Ott, who was playing bass guitar.

Of course I knew who the boy was, and so did Bro. Ott. It was his grandson, Chris. Chris lives in Sulphur and was not known by many of our players. As he set up his gear, we were already into the next set of songs. Several of the older players suspiciously eyed Chris with his green hair and baggy clothes. I thought to myself, "Guys, you're going to be surprised when "green hair" starts playing!

Chris sat on the piano bench and started strumming along. Then he started picking leads on every song. Many of the songs he had obviously never heard, especially the older songs. On the first verse he'd listen quizzically with the wonderful God-given musical ear he'd been given. Then by the second verse, he always had it and led the charge among the guitar players.

I wondered what it was like inside the mind of this gifted musician as he heard with his ear what seconds later he could play on the guitar. The older guys' suspicious looks turned to astonishment. Finally, after Chris had played about five songs, Bro. Ott said, "Men, this is my grandson, Chris Harper."

During our next break, the guitar players all gathered around swapping ideas and licks. It was so moving to see veteran players like Julian and Vance, sharing tips with the eager young players. These older men would laugh at the young guys with their distortion pedals, big amps, and more radical playing styles. Nevertheless, there was a readily apparent bond, regardless of the ages, styles, and yes, even the hairstyle. I could see and feel the bond of respect developing between these three generations of players who really only had one thing in common- a love of playing music. I was once again reminded of the unbroken circle of music. The styles change, and the instruments sometimes get louder. Each generation develops its own way of expressing itself musically. But the unbroken circle of deep love for music lives on, generation after generation.

Over time our repertoire began to grow. Most of what we'd sang in the past were songs twenty years old or older. Now, after singing several traditional old hymns, one of the young guys would break into a praise chorus, the type of song so popular with our younger generation. All of these songs, although different in style, were common in that they gave praise to the Lord.

Then another special thing happened. Toward the end of last year, my youngest son Terry began playing guitar. He practiced day after day for hours. It was pretty ragged at first, but soon recognizable chords began to emerge. At one of our next singings, Terry sat by Bro. Frank Ott strumming along, as the "Preacher" (That is what most people call Frank Ott) patiently called out the chords and changes to him for over two hours.

Beside Terry sat Aubrey Cole, one of our area's best-known bluegrass fiddlers. Some of my earliest musical memories are watching Mr. Aubrey play at singings like this one. After all of these years, there is still a special smile and glow on Mr. Aubrey's face as he draws his bow across the fiddle strings.

Mr. Aubrey Cole with his fiddle

As Mr. Aubrey plays, he smiles as he watches Terry. Across the room, Mr. Aubrey's grandson, Cody, plays along on the piano. What a special moment it is as this man, nearly eighty-years old, patiently plays with these young guys.

This long musical legacy is brought home to me by a statement from Mr. Aubrey during one of our breaks. He leans over to twelve-year old Terry, and kindly tells him,

"Son, when I was a young fiddle player your great-great grandma used to beat me every year at the Parish Fair fiddling contest."

The idea that Mr. Aubrey had played with "Doten," probably over sixty years ago, and was now playing with her great-great grandson said so much about the rich legacy, and that unbroken circle of music. This country fiddler was now playing music with the fifth generation of my family. . . The rich legacy of music continues.

However, there is one night I believe I will remember when all of the other singings have been forgotten. This took place on a Monday night in March 2001. A group of northern volunteers were helping on a work project at the camp. As a way of saying thanks, and to introduce them to the culture of southern music, we hosted a singing at the camp.

The week before, my dad had discovered some lumps in his groin and armpit. His doctor was concerned and began testing immediately to check these out. We all knew this could be cancer and had no idea if it was, where else it might be located. He had a cat scan done and waited for word on the outcome.

The following week, he still had received no results from these tests. Earlier we had scheduled this Monday night singing. I told Daddy not to come to the singing unless he felt like it. All throughout that long day I waited for the news from his tests.

After supper that evening, he showed up ready to sing. When I asked him if he'd heard from the doctor's office, he replied that he had not, but expected them to call later that evening. He'd left the camp number with the Doctor's office so they could reach him.

Our time singing was special - all of our best singers and players were there. The guitars, keyboard, fiddle, and drums just blended together in a special way. There is no other feeling quite like when the music just comes together and takes you all along for a ride. It was that kind of magical night.

We'd been singing about thirty minutes when they called my mom out of the room. She motioned to my dad and he left the microphone to join her. I knew in my heart of hearts that a phone call informing my dad of either good news or bad news awaited him next door. I continued playing my drums, but my playing was listless and mechanical. My mind was on my dad and mom next door. We continued playing for several more songs. The wait seemed forever to me.

Then my dad and mom came in the back door. Dad's expression looked just the same as when he'd left. He stepped right back to the microphone and resumed singing. But when I looked at my mom's face, with tears streaming down her cheeks, I knew without words, the prognosis had been cancer.

However, you'd never have known it watching my dad. In fact, he had a special spring to his step and an added passion in his voice. As we sang some of those old songs about Heaven, he just seemed to reach out to another level as he sang about the joys of being in God's presence.

I'll never forget that night. My dad's singing, determination, and faith were not tied to his circumstances or health, but his faith in Jesus, the Solid Rock. His body might have lymphoma, but his spirit was alive and healthy. I thought to myself, this will be a long journey we all are going to be on, but I know we'll get through it with my

God's strength, my dad's determination, and the support of our family.

In the midst of that emotional night, I vowed to myself as to how we'd have as many singings as possible in the coming months... I was reminded that none of us know when we may have the last opportunity to sing together and enjoy the common bond of music. Beginning that night, we began having more frequent singings. Many weekends, when Daddy was not too sick from chemotherapy, we'd get together and sing.

Tonight is one of those nights. We've played for over three hours. For the last thirty minutes we've said, "Now, this is our last song," but someone always calls out "just one more." I can see my dad is tired, but I believe this singing is just as important as his chemo. Finally after a wonderful evening of playing, we begin loading up our equipment. Julian lets each of the young guys strum on his collector's item Gibson Chet Atkins Model guitar. As the cords and wires are packed up, guitars are cased, and amps are carried to vehicles, I begin breaking down my drum set. Everyone has that happy and satisfied look of guys who've reached deep down into their souls and did what they love to do- play songs together in the bond of music. There is a growing feeling of respect from our entire group for the other styles of music that all praise our Lord.

Before the guys start heading out the door, I look around...there are men and young men from four different generations. As always, there are different Christian denominations. A quick look around the room reveals vastly different hairstyles: from the shaggy, highlighted, and spiked hair of our teenagers to my dad's shaved head and Mr. Aubrey's white hair. The boys in their baggy clothing, which is their generation's fashion statement, and we older guys in our normal uniforms- blue jeans. Our backgrounds, jobs, and education are varied. The group's preferred styles of music is without a doubt as varied as the four winds.

But all of these differences don't really matter when we join together in the wonderful common bond of music, that unbroken circle of each successive generation and their music. There is a commonality that we take with us from this night. From now on those of us, who tonight were part of something bigger than ourselves, will always remember the wonderful and unbreakable bond of music.

Taught by Teenagers

"And my God shall supply all of your needs according to His glorious riches in Christ Jesus."
Philippians 4:19

I've come to the simple conclusion that young people can teach us much more than we could ever teach them. This is a story of what several teens have taught me in the last two years.

One of the greatest promises in God's word is found in Paul's writings in Romans. In chapter 8, he lets his readers know that God can take *all* things and bring good out of *everything that* happens to us:

And we know that all things work together for good, for those who love God, and are the called according to His purpose.
Romans 8:28

I'm no theologian, but I take every verse of the Bible as God-revealed truth, especially the great promises found throughout scripture. The promise of Romans 8:28 is probably my favorite. It is a solid promise that we can build our lives and faith on. I like to call it "the rock solid promise" for building a strong foundation in life.

I want to be honest- I don't understand exactly why God, who knows all things before they happen, allows some of the tragedies that come to us as we travel on life's journey.

You'll notice I didn't say God *causes* bad things to occur. Nothing in my experience, or the scriptures, point to God causing evil or trouble. However, He does *allow* some things to pass through the protective hedge He has placed around us.

To believe God did not have dominance and veto power over evil would be to deny the complete authority of God over everything, including evil.

On Friday, September 14, three days after the terrorist attacks on our nation, President Bush called for a national day of prayer. That morning, our entire nation stopped and watched the prayer service held at the National Cathedral in Washington. It was a touching and memorable service as four former presidents sat together with President George Bush, as they joined millions in prayer for America.

The defining moment of the service was when the Dr. Rev. Billy Graham came forward to speak. The aged Dr. Graham, now very feeble, was helped to the podium. As he silently stood there, it was if the entire cathedral and our entire nation held its breath to hear what this highly respected man of God had to say.

When he spoke his first words, he no longer seemed old and frail. The strong voice and forceful presence we've loved for over fifty years came forth with full power. Early in his speech, he made a comment that made me lean forward expectantly toward the TV screen.

"Many of you have asked me to, 'Why did God allow this to happen?' "

I thought to myself, "Finally, we are going to hear and understand why God allows terrible tragedies to occur." After a brief hesitation, Billy Graham continued, "I have to tell you that I don't really know."

Here was this special man of God, probably the most respected Christian in the world. A man who had faithfully preached and been powerfully used by God for his entire life. Here he was admitting that he did not fully understand this tragedy either.

Then I recalled the words of Charles Hadden Spurgeon, the great English evangelist,

God is too great to be confused,
And too kind to be cruel,
So when I can't trace His hand,
I simply must trust His heart

You see, following and obeying God has never been a vaccination against hard times. Jesus himself said that His followers would receive hardship,

"I have told you these things, so that in me you may have peace. In this world you will have trouble. But take heart! I have overcome the world."
John 16:33

Additionally he reminded us that the rain falls on the just and unjust. None of us are exempt from the trial and tragedies of life. Christians experience this same combination of blessings and trials, and joy followed by deep sorrow, in their lives as non-believers. Those who follow Jesus still get cancer, have car accidents, get laid off, and lose loved ones through illness and accidents. But there is a difference- Our God stands with us during these times of trouble. He never forsakes us but instead gives the comfort and peace that passes all understanding.

And He promises, in Romans 8:28, that He will, in time, bring about good through all things we experience. I want to emphasize that the Bible says *all* things. Not some things, but in each and every event and occurrence. It's as one of my friends reminds me, "All means all and that is all all means"

"All also means in His time. Our problem is often our timetable is not the same as God's. Our great God is eternal and infinite. Time means nothing to him. He is not bound by, nor does her ever feel rushed or panicked, by finite time.

As humans, we only see things in our temporary time-oriented mind set. Everything we experience- whether a good movie, a delicious meal, a lifelong marriage, and finally even the end of our lives- all of these earthly events have a beginning and an ending.

Therefore when we wonder where God is, and why He hasn't stepped forward yet, we must trust God's timetable and realize he is not slow nor has he forgotten us. We'll do well to remember this wise saying, "There is never a panic in heaven, God always has a plan."

I must realize that some of my earthly questions may not fully be answered until Heaven, but I do believe I will receive a full accounting from God at that time.

I've always loved the old hymn that soars with its inspiring chorus:

"By and by, when the morning comes,
By and by, when the saints are gathered home.
We will tell the story of how we've overcome,
We will understand it better by and by."[1]

Yes, Romans 8:28 assures us that all things work together for those who love and serve God. All of these things, both joyful and painful, are blended together to produce a more Christ-like person and a steadiness and confidence to face any obstacle.

Picture a cook in the kitchen mixing ingredients together to make a cake. Some of the ingredients are untasty, but are an essential part of the cake recipe. As a child, I loved to sit and watch as my mother made a cake. I expectantly awaited my job, which was to lick the delicious and sweet leftover cake mix from the bowl. I'd watch her mix baking powder, flour, raw eggs, chocolate, and sugar together, knowing the end result would not be just a tasty bowl to lick, but delicious cake for dessert after supper.

---

[1] When the Morning Comes, Southern Melody arranged by B.B. McKinney

Once out of curiosity, I decided to try out the taste of the baking powder I'd seen mom mixing into the cake mix. Because the sweet cake mix tasted so good, I thought for sure the powder would too. I got a quick lesson in bitter tastes that day. As I spit it out, I asked my mom a question, "Now, how could a mixture so sweet in the end, contain an ingredient so bitter and untasty?"

That is exactly what God does in our lives. He takes the joys, sorrows, hurts, blessings, and disappointments and mixes them together to bring about good in our lives. What often seems accidental, or coincidence, is really the hand of God doing his quiet, yet powerful, work in us.

In the past two years, I've had two very special young people teach me about this principle of God bringing good out of so-called "accidents."

Marcie is a senior at our school this year. To be honest, and she'd be the first to agree, her life over the previous year had been traumatic and tough. I also believe she would concur that much of her trouble was the result of poor decisions.

However, about six months before her senior year started, God began a fresh work in Marcie's life. Through a variety of circumstances, God began to tenderly call her back to Him. As spring moved toward summer, I talked with her about serving as a lifeguard at the camp pool. I knew she'd be a good lifeguard and I also felt that it would be a great experience for her spiritually as she would be at the camp a great deal.

You should have seen her face when I asked her. She was thrilled about the opportunity of this job. But I really believe what thrilled her most was the fact that someone believed in her enough to ask her to fill one of our most important jobs.

As May arrived, and school came to a close, Marcie and our other lifeguards completed their rigorous training at the city pool in DeRidder. They had to perform tasks things such as treading water for fifteen minutes and carrying out all types of rescue drills. It was a tough time of training that pushed them to their limits. As I knew she would, Marcie passed. I had seen enough of her on the basketball court to know how tough and determined she was when there was a goal to reach.

Summer started and we all became busy in all of our respective responsibilities. Summer camp is a wonderful time of great fun, spiritual victories, and the beauty of seeing hundreds of youth experiencing God in a special way. It thrilled me to see Marcie join us for the nightly services. It was evident a new spiritual hunger was burning within her.

So often we try to change people externally by verbal or physical methods. I've learned that only the power of Jesus can change a heart... and that is what I saw God doing internally in Marcie's life. I just believe with so many people were praying for Marcie, there was no way she wasn't going to be drawn toward Jesus.

The end of June approached. We now had three weeks of camp under our belt. On Sunday, June 24 our first youth camp began. Afternoon registration was going full force, and the excitement of hundreds of campers descending on the grounds made the air thick with anticipation. You could tell there was a sense of expecting God to really work this week.

In the midst of all this, someone slipped up to me and whispered, "Marcie has been in a bad wreck on the curve near Pederson's. She's conscious, but it's a terrible crash." Our pastor, Don Hunt, and I rushed to the scene of the accident. As we rounded the sharp curve where the accident was, an air med helicopter was landing in a nearby open field.

The sobering sight of Marcie's gray car wrapped around a large pine tree will live with me forever. I've seen many car accidents, but never one where a vehicle was as crumpled as her car was. It looked as if her northbound car had swerved over into the opposite ditch and hit this good-sized pine tree in mid air as the car began to flip. The car was literally bent around the tree and the roof was crumpled in. Someone later told me that the first ambulance driver to arrive had asked the question, "Are there any survivors?"

I saw Mary, Marcie's mother standing there as medical personnel took care of Marcie, who lay trapped in the car. Her dad, Ted, knelt beside the shattered car, amid the broken glass, as he firmly held Marcie's hand.

Surveying the scene, I knew what my job was- go stand beside Mary. Through the tough times of Marcie's painful recent journey, I had been Mary's prayer partner. I knew this was an essential time for everyone's prayer support and the simple ministry of just being there for those whom we love.

The impact had shoved Marcie over to the passenger side of the front seat. She was badly hurt but conscious. The car lay on its side with her side being down. She hung there in the only part of the vehicle that wasn't crushed down flat. To her left, the roof was just a few inches from the steering wheel. But Marcie was going to survive as far as we could see. It took a long and painful time to extricate her from the car. Then they rushed her to the helicopter which quickly flew away to Lake Charles.

Going back to my truck, I thanked God as to how He had chosen to spare Marcie's life. I asked God to reveal to her what He had in store for her in the future through this experience.

In the coming week, as I watched a week of youth camp unfold, Marcie's accident would not leave my mind. At the time of the accident, Marcie was returning home from my niece's house where she'd had her hair highlighted. From there she was coming to camp for the week. When camp ended, she was going to South Dakota on a mission trip.

However, the accident had suddenly changed all of this. Among her worst injuries were a broken pelvis in two places, a collapsed lung, and a chipped vertebra in her neck. Her dream of playing basketball her senior year was gone. Gone also was the normal life that she had been living prior to June 24.

Her pelvic injuries were due to the seat belt holding her in place at the terrific point of impact. The force was so great that one of the seat belt anchors broke loose. This was the reason Marcie was pushed to the passenger side of the front seat. Some may call it coincidence, but I fully believe God spared her life, because the driver's side is where the maximum impact occurred.

I've been at accidents where there was minimal vehicle damage, but great injuries or death. Then I've seen wrecks like this where no one should have survived, but they did. None of those at Marcie's accident, from the policeman to the medical personnel, could really explain how Marcie escaped with her life.

Marcie stayed several days in Lake Charles Memorial Hospital and then was transferred to Tulane Hospital in New Orleans. There she underwent a nine-hour operation on her pelvic injuries. Eventually she returned home after nearly two weeks in two hospitals.

The day after she came home, I went to visit her. Driving there, I rounded the curve where the accident had occurred. Some of her friends had put a large sign on the pine tree Marcie hit. It simply read, "Thank you God for sparing Marcie's life." The poster was signed by several of her closest friends.

I drove on to her house. Visiting a young person who has been in a serious accident is a sobering experience.

There Marcie lay there in a hospital bed in the living room of her home. A home health nurse was checking her out as Mary Allen stood watching nearby.

As I went to her bedside, the light in her eyes caught my attention more than her injuries and the medical equipment arranged around the room. There was a peace that exuded from her which I knew could only be from God, and due to her gratitude in being alive.

We visited and this bright smile stayed on her face. Our conversation drifted to God's promise in Romans 8:28 and the assurance as to how He would bring good out of any situation. I listened carefully because I knew I had no right to interpret the good that was going to come about because of Marcie's accident.

Discovering the good is a very personal decision that takes different amounts of time for each individual. Marcie's words confirmed how she was already looking for the good from being flat on her back in a hospital bed. She shared,

"Yesterday, I saw how God is already using this for good. When I arrived home late last night from New Orleans, my grandfather was waiting here for me. All of my life, I've especially loved him and knew he loves me just as much. But he's never been able to easily express how deeply he felt to me."

I pictured her grandfather, a highly decorated World War II veteran. Often the men of this generation, that weathered the Great Depression and saved the world in Europe and the Pacific, don't always express their feelings and emotions easily.

Marcie continued, "Last night, my grandfather came to my bedside and for the first time in my life expressed deeply and with touching emotion how much he loved me."

Once again a look of peace settled over Marcie. Next, she made one of the most profound statement I've ever heard a teenager (or even an adult) say,

"Bro. Curt, to hear my grandfather say what he did, made every bit of this accident worth it all."

I stared in amazement at Marcie. Here she was recovering from a close encounter with death. She was laying in a bed where she would be for a long time. Her senior year of school would be different from what she'd planned. Her basketball-playing career seemed to be over. Yet in all of this, she was already beginning to see the good coming forth.

Later Marcie wrote a poem which she gave me permission to share. These touching words, entitled "Trapped. . . Free," come from her experiences of the last year,

Walking	Wheelchairbound
Seemingly free	Seemingly trapped
Surrounded by losers	Surrounded by encouragers
Stripped of self esteem	Nurtured by the those who love
Impatient	Thankful
Defiant	Content
Considers self a disappointment	Realizes worth
Back turned to God	Face to face with the Cross
Trapped	Free

After reading these words and seeing the strides made by Marcie both physically and spiritually, I once again thanked God for allowing me to work with young people. I'm convinced that they are the best teachers we will ever have.

However, there is one more chapter to add to Marcie's story. Later in the fall of 2001, the Allen family home burned. Every material thing they possessed was lost. Marcie was not home the night of the fire. Mary Allen told me that when she went to tell Marcie the bad news,

Marcie's only concern was for her sister Veronica being safe. She commented on the loss of all of her possessions with this statement,

"Those are only things and they can be replaced. I'm just thankful you, dad, and Veronica are all right." Once again, this teenager became a teacher for all of us.

A few months later, Marcie brought me a gift that I will cherish until the day I die. It is a framed mosaic. The glass in the mosaic is in the form of the cross. The text reads,

Life is fragile as glass.
Only the Cross lasts for Eternity.

However, there was something else that made this gift so precious:

The glass pieces making up the cross were a mixture of windshield glass from Marcie's accident and the windows of their home. You could see the fire damage on the shards from the house. I still stare in humility at this visual testimony of God growing a young person to a new spiritual maturity that all of us could learn from.

Then I thought about my greatest teacher of this past year- my son Clint. Like Marcie, Clint is a senior this school year. Like his two brothers, Clint loves sports and has worked very hard at anything he has ever attempted.

Last year, his junior year of high school, Clint finally achieved one of his goals- he was the starting quarterback for the football team. During the team's third game against Merryville, Clint kept the ball on an option play and ran for a nice gain.

When he was tackled and the players unpiled, Clint lay still on the ground. I knew he was hurt badly, because he usually is up quickly whether he's been hit hard or not. I'll never forget the total silence of the crowd as he lay prone on the field. When DeDe and I saw him moving his legs, I felt a little better. After a long time, which seemed forever, they began preparing to move him. I had hesitated going down on the field because our boys had always said, "Daddy, if I get hurt, don't come running down there and embarrass me." At this point, his mother and I really didn't care about hurting his feelings.

As they carried him off the field to the ambulance, my heart just sank. It was evident Clint had some type of serious hip injury. Just before they loaded him into the ambulance, he told his coach, "Coach, I read that play right, didn't I? They covered the tailback and I kept it for that good run."

I knew then that this fighter was going to overcome his injury. This first ambulance ride was one of three we would take over the next several days. Clint had a badly dislocated hip. From Merryville, we went to the hospital in DeRidder. Because of the seriousness of the accident, Clint was transferred that night to the hospital in Lake Charles.

Eventually, we ended up in Houston at Methodist Hospital, one of the finest facilities in the world. It was here that Clint began his long journey back from this injury. In his room was a dry erase marker board. On it, I drew the picture of a football player running with the ball, wearing Clint's number 12. Below it I wrote, "Next time pitch the ball!" Even through the pain, he grinned his wonderful smile that has always been one of the lights of my life.

You've never seen anyone work harder than he did to rehabilitate his hip. He swam long hours and rode an exercise bike mile after mile. Slowly he began to regain his mobility. By February he was able to begin practicing for the upcoming high school baseball season.

I don't want it to sound as if the only thing Clint, or his parents, wanted was for him to play sports again. Our greatest prayer was for Clint to regain full use of his hip so he could have a healthy life. We wanted to see him be able to go on future hiking trips, skiing, and one day play with his children without pain.

The most remarkable thing about this time was not his physical progress, but the spiritual growth we saw in his life. I was reminded once again that young people often teach us our most important lessons and many times these lessons are taught through trying circumstances.

We knew that Clint was hurting inside, but he kept going and working hard. Most of all, we all recognized the growth in his walk with Christ. As the second sentence of Romans 8:29 states, God was using "all things for good"...to conform Clint to be more like Jesus. "For all things work together for the good of them that love the Lord . . . to be conformed to the image of Christ." Romans 8:28, 29

Just as with Marcie, God was using all of the circumstances in a young life to shape a person to be more like Him. When we are in the midst of trouble and trials, God will pour us into the "Jesus mold" to shape us to become more like His Son.

A picture of working with ceramics comes to mind. The worker takes the plaster of paris and mixes it with water. Then this thick liquid is poured into a mold. The shape of this mold determines the shape of the ceramic object. After the molded object hardens, it is removed from the mold and placed in a large oven called a kiln. Prior to this heating process, this ceramic object is brittle and breaks easily. However, after spending hours in the intense heat of the kiln, the ceramic piece that comes out of the oven is both hard and usable.

I think this is an apt analogy for what God has been doing in Marcie and Clint's lives. God uses everything in our lives to shape us in the Jesus mold. We come out of the mold shaped to be more like Him. And this "heating process" of adversity, which we usually run from, results in a toughness and resilience that can withstand whatever comes our way.

As I write this, Marcie is progressing well on her recovery. Believe it or not, she has been able to return to play high school basketball. It's now been over a year and a half since Clint's accident. He continues to have some pain and still has a limp. In addition, this summer, Clint had shoulder surgery for a torn ligament that was allowing his shoulder joint to repeatedly pop out of place. It's like his doctor said when he diagnosed his shoulder, "Buddy, you're living kind of rough, aren't you?"

This doctor's visit clearly showed Clint his football career was over. I just wanted to pick him up and hug him, but that's not what you do with a seventeen-year old in public. The disappointment of this after he had worked so hard all spring and summer to return to the field. was hard to take. However, Clint took the prognosis calmly.

Later, he told me about his feelings on this matter. Once again, it was time for me to be taught by a teenager: "Daddy, I'm so disappointed that I won't be able to play football. But even with my disappointment, I have a strange peace about it. I know it is going to work out for good and God's plans won't be stopped."

Clint reassured me as to his commitment to be a vital part of the football team as a non-playing senior. He wanted to see how God would use him on the team as a witness. Tears freely flowed down my cheeks as he shared. I know I never would have handled this when I was a teenager and I was touched, humbled, and so thankful for the lesson I was being taught by my own son. I can honestly say that if he'd played and led his team to the championship, I could not have been prouder.

I don't understand why things happen as they do. Why one car accident takes the life of a vibrant teen, while in when another accident, with much more damage, the driver is only slightly injured. I don't have an answer as to why some guys play football for years with no serious injuries, yet my son, who was working hard and trying to be a witness for God, had a serious injury that ended his career and has resulted in a long time of immobility.

I think back to the Godly saints whom I've seen handle tribulation with grace and patience. Instead of becoming bitter and resentful toward God, they only grew closer to Him, and reached down deeper into His love.

This grace was best illustrated to me by my friends, Bubba and Karan Robinson. As I shared earlier in this book, the death of their son Brad saddened and grieved so many people all across our part of Louisiana. I've never understood why God allowed a speeding car, driven recklessly for miles, to finally crash into Brad's truck, resulting in his death. As I talked to God about Brad's death in the weeks following his accident, I asked God for an explanation. I didn't ask it angrily, but I still believe He would not have struck me down, even if I had asked in anger and pain.

Here was my heartfelt question, "Why, God, would you allow the tragic death of a young man sold out to you and committed to preaching your gospel for the rest of his life? How could you allow this to happen?"

I didn't get killed by a lightning bolt, because I believe our Heavenly Father wants us to come to Him honestly with our feelings. But neither did I get an answer right then. Finally, only after time had passed, and as healing started in my heart, did I hear the still small voice of the Holy Spirit as He replied to my question. It reminds me of the question referred to a man who had just shared about hearing God's voice. The second man asked him, "Did He speak to you verbally where you could hear him?"

The first man smiled and replied, "No, it was much louder than that."

Here's what God's sweet spirit began telling me deep down in my heart: "One day you will see the reason for this. It will take time. You may not even fully understand it in this life, but one day in my presence you'll know the reason, and all of the resulting good that came out of it."

. . . Moreover, that was all I needed to hear. I was able to move on in my journey of the process of grief. Since that time I've asked God "why" about many unreasonable hardships and tragedies I've seen. However, I have the sneaking suspicion that one day when I enter the presence of God, and see the Jesus I've sought to serve and follow for all of my life, I won't need an explanation. Just to be in His presence, and yes to be reunited with loved ones such as Brad, will make it all clear.

I firmly believe in Romans 8:28 for my life and the lives of others who love God- All things can, and will, be used for good. I don't know the future joys and trials that await me on the long and bumpy road of life. All I know is that my God will stand faithfully beside me through it all, and He will use every event for His glory and my growth.

About a year after Brad's death, Karan Robinson made a very profound statement to DeDe and me. Here is what she shared, "You know I miss Brad so bad and would do anything to see him again. However, God has made it so clear to me as to how He is continuing to bring good from Brad's life, and yes, even from his death. So much good has come from all of this, and so many lives have been changed that there is no way I can be unhappy."

I couldn't reply to Karan because I had no right to speak in the presence of someone so tuned in to God. The peace on her face and the light in her eyes clearly showed she meant what she'd just said.

I thought about all of the victories we've continued to see due to the spreading testimony of Brad Robinson's life: web sites celebrating his life, tracts reminding you to "B.R.A.D.," which stands for "Be Ready At Death." The basketball court bearing his name at the camp, which is used non-stop by our campers, and the sign at the court bearing witness to Brad's testimony.

Then I think of the young men who were Brad's best friends, many of whom have chosen to walk deeper in God's love. Many of them are moving toward the same gospel ministry Brad felt called to. The ever-spreading circle of stories of Brad's life, even two years after his death, continues to touch others in a widening circle of ripples. Yes, even the fact that here on the pages of this book, readers like you, from all over our nation and even the world, can read this testimony to Brad's life. You can also know that this promise of God, to use all the events of your life for good, is a promise you can "take to the bank" and build your life while loving God in a deep and more intimate way.

I thank God for teaching these lessons to me through young people. I recall the words of the great French scientist Louis Pasteur:

"When I see a young person I experience two strong emotions- First of all, I feel great affection for the young person they are. Then secondly, I feel a deep respect for the adult they will one day become."

And as I reflect on all of this, Brad's life, Marcie's accident, and Clint's injury, I'm so thankful to serve the wonderful God we serve. A God so powerful that He can take any event and use it for our good and the work of His kingdom. Now that is a great and powerful God, whom I want to know, serve and trust.

Sliding into Home...with no Regrets

Twenty years from now, you will be more disappointed by things you didn't do than by the ones you did. So throw off the bowlines, sail away from the safe harbor. Catch the trade winds in your sails. Explore. Dream.
- *Mark Twain*

As I'm sitting here writing, I'm nursing a very sore leg. It's propped up on the wooden banister at my Old House writing spot. My left leg, from below my knee to my ankle is one long red abrasion. I've got what we call in sports a "slide burn" or a "strawberry." As I look down at my leg, it does resemble a strawberry.

Last Sunday was Father's Day. As a special present for me, DeDe and the boys surprised me with tickets for all of us to travel to Houston to watch the Astros and Texas Rangers play baseball.

There is nothing I enjoy more than a good baseball game, especially when I'm going with my family. To sit in the stands and just soak in the atmosphere of a major league game is something I've always loved. And whether it is because of heredity or environment, my three boys enjoy playing and watching baseball together as much as I do.

After all these years, DeDe has grown to love the game too. Through hundreds of games from T-ball to high school games, she has been a faithful fan and supporter of her sons. I think she is excited about going to Enron Field for this game. However, I can tell she is most excited about surprising me and the joy of the day we will spend together as a family.

She always makes fun of me and my insistence that we arrive early. She swears we are at the park even before the vendors arrive. I always reply, "If you are going to drive this far to see a game, you should get every bit of your money's worth."

Houston is three hours from our home. As always, we get an early start for this afternoon game. We have a family rule to arrive at the park in time to see batting practice. The trip passes quickly as we visit and enjoy each other's company. I think of how precious and priceless this time together is for the five of us. With a son in college and another set to graduate, it is harder to get us all together at one time. So, I'm going to attempt to make time slow down and just drink in this special day.

Upon arrival at Enron Field, we stand just outside the entrance waiting for the gates to open. This is only the second season for Enron Field. Prior to that the Astros played at the Astrodome for over thirty years.

My boys thought there was only one place to see a baseball game, and it was at the Astrodome. When the season ended and Enron field was set to be open, it felt as if we were losing a longtime friend. The boys were very skeptical about this new park.

However, during the 2000 season we saw several games and grew to love this new ballpark. Baseball is a game meant to be played on grass, not Astroturf, and it was good to see the sky from a major league stadium. Today, as we stand in line eager to get in, we hope they will have the retractable roof open.

All around us are fans just as excited as we are. Most are dressed in Astros colors, but a good number sport the logo and colors of the Texas Rangers. This is the first year these two Texas teams have played in the regular season, due to their being in different leagues.

After what seems forever, the gates open, and we hurry in to get strategic locations for snagging balls during batting practice. Terry goes down to the stands along the dugout hoping to get an autograph. Already there is a growing excitement in the park as other early arrivals stream into the park.

Finally, we settle into our seats, while enjoying a high-priced ballpark lunch. There's something about a hot dog at a ballpark. It just tastes better, even if it's washed down with a three-dollar coke.

The game is a good one. A record crowd of over forty thousand fans packs the stands. Judging from the crowd noise, the Astros have most of the fans, but the Ranger faithful hold their own. On this day, their team leads 6-2 late in the game.

Toward the eighth inning, many fans begin leaving to beat the traffic. Clay, Clint, and Terry always shake their heads in amazement. Twelve-year-old Terry asks "Why would anyone want to leave a ball game early?" Beside me DeDe, rolls her eyes and says in my ear, "These guys really do have baseball on the brain and I know right where they got it."

With the final out we stand and stretch contemplating the long journey home. Just as we start up the ramp from our seats, the public address announces, "*All right, dads this is your special day. Come on down because all fathers get to run the bases*."

All four members of my family look at me. My first impulse is to say, "Look, we are going to be late even as it is, I think we'll skip this." Then the thought hits me, "If I don't run those bases today on that field, I'll probably never get another chance."

As I'm struggling with this, my mind flashes back to when Clay and Clint were small. We went to a game at the Astrodome, and they allowed all of the kids to run the bases. It was a sight to see. Boys and girls of all ages ran the bases. Some dressed in uniforms, others in jeans. Some toddlers, others too small to play T-ball, ran the bases with reckless abandon, sliding at each base before getting up and running to the next one.

I think to myself, "I'm forty-five-years old and I know I'll look pretty silly out there running in my shorts and loose fitting sandals" But then another thought collided with the previous one. I said to myself, "If I don't run those bases, I'll regret it to my dying day. It's something I've always wanted to do... and I'm going for it."

With that I hand my camera and daypack to DeDe. The boys all laugh as they realize I'm going for it. As I head toward section 134 where the line forms, there is a huge mass of people blocking each exit so that anyone crossing through must carefully wade through "swimming upstream" against the crowd. At the first jammed exit, I start to turn around and go back to my family. It just seems as if the time and trouble to run the bases isn't worth it.

But I keep asking myself if I'll regret it if I don't follow through. Finally, I get to the long line of men snaking down onto the field. Many men are just like me in that they are not going to pass up the chance of a lifetime.

As our line slowly moves through the stands onto to the actual field, it seems as if we'll never get there. A woman tries to sneak into line and a security guard makes her leave with the words, "I'm sorry, Ma'am, but this is the men's day." I start to add, "Come back next Mother's Day and you can then," but thinking better, I remain quiet.

As we creep along I enjoy watching the men of every size, and age, running the bases at Enron Field. Many are younger men, stepping high as they relive their athletic careers. Other men run and you can tell they are living out their fantasy as they score and help the Astros win the biggest game of the year.

One particular runner catches my attention. He is an old man, gray headed, and bent over from what looks to be over eighty years of living. He is accompanied by both his trusty walking cane and a man at his elbow, who looks to be his son. This old man, who probably came to love the game of baseball during the days of heyday of Babe Ruth and Ty Cobb, takes small steps and several minutes to tour the bases.

As the line moves down and my turn nears, I make a plan. Since this is probably my only opportunity to ever do this, I'm going to slide at home plate. Once again the two voices collide in my mind. Safe Curt says, "Don't do it. You'll just look silly." Nevertheless "Adventuresome Curt" answers back, "Go for it. You only go around once in life and this is your chance." I remember that old commercial of my younger days, "You only go around once in life, so you've got to grab all of the gusto you can."

So I tell myself, "Go for it." When my time comes, I get a short lead off first, and then I take off for second. I just hope I beat the catcher's throw. Then I round second headed for third. There I run up on two slow fat men. They are running side by side and I can't go around them without going out of the base path. So, I slow down as I near third. It's at that point that I hear my boys calling from the stands, "Slide, daddy, slide." They've come down on the third base side to cheer me on.

As I approach the plate, I think about how grainy the cinder is which they use on a major league field. I know my shorts won't protect my legs. Once again it is a crisis point in my mind. I even consider a halfway slide to appease both voices in my head.

But I know I must slide the only way I know- full speed and all out. And that's just what I do. I glide through the dirt with my left leg tucked under my right. I hit the plate and get up as quickly as my body will allow me. An Astros official, standing at the plate to keep runners from stealing dirt or grass, loudly signals me out and gives me the thumb in dramatic fashion as he loudly says, "You're outta there. Now keep on going."

As I brush the dirt off my behind, I tell this 'ump,' "No way ump, I got under that tag." It's a good feeling as I walk through the stands to catch up with my family. As I look down at my leg, I begin to brush the cinders and dirt off my leg.

My leg is slightly bloody and stings like crazy. However, I know I would do it again and do it in exactly the same way. As we walk to our vehicle, I think about how many times I've avoided risks because of too much concern as to what others would say or think. How many times have I avoided "sliding" because I might get called out, or worse-ridiculed and scoffed at.

As I've gotten older, I rely less and less on playing it safe because of fear of looking stupid. As the days and years go by, the Latin term, "Carpe Diem" which means, "Seize the day" resounds in my mind.

During the latter part of 2000, I went through the toughest time of my life. I spent over three months stuck in terrible depression. It reached the point where I could not work and do the many things I had always enjoyed. Even though I had this long amount of free time, I could not write. My soul felt as if it had dried up, and there would never be any joy or creativity in me again.

Finally, I slowly began coming out of this dark time, due to the prayers and support of so many folks, and the knowledgeable care of my doctors, coupled with the medications available to treat depression. As I began to heal and regain my joy of living, I noticed an additional change that was good: I was less concerned with what others thought and more concerned with living each precious moment as God allowed me the privilege of being alive.

Just the fact that I'm writing openly about this ordeal tells me that I've lost some of the shackles of worrying about the approval of others. I've found great freedom in being loosed from this heavy load. Because everyone in our community and area knew about my struggle with depression, I realized I didn't have to try to look like Superman, or act as if I had no problems and challenges.

People see me now and realize that I'm just another fellow traveler struggling along this road of life. Instead of thinking what will others think, I'm now learning to say, "What is really most important to me today and how can I best enjoy life and serve my God?"

I've found that many times where I would previously have taken the safe route and barely touched the plate as I ran by; I now know the importance of "sliding into home." My mind set now is "Will I regret not doing this down the road?"

It means lovingly tending our many relationships. Steven Covey in his excellent book, *First Things First* states, "No man on his deathbed has ever said, "I wish I'd spent more time at the office, but many men have lamented at not spending time with, and investing in, their families."

"No regret" living is not a license to do as we please and hurt others or ourselves. Trying to live with no regrets is simply doing whatever is important each day. Just as importantly, it also means not doing anything we would regret later.

Sliding home with no regrets- It's what I want to do in my life, everyday and in every way.

A Friendship Fire

It's a beautiful March night. During this third month of the year, the nights are cool and the days are normally mild. The blossoms of spring begin to show off- the azaleas, dogwoods, and honeysuckle. Most of the days are full of blue skies and moderate temperatures. Best of all, the mosquitoes haven't become a nightly nuisance.

Therefore, I hunt for every chance I can to be outside in March. It's a great month for my youngest son, Terry, and I to build what we call a "Friendship Fire." I'm not sure where the name came from, but I believe Terry, age twelve, came up with it. Often, he will come to me and say, "Daddy, let's build a friendship fire tonight."

We'll venture out behind our house in the edge of the field. It is far enough from the lights that the darkness is deep and the sky reveals itself on clear nights. In the field is an area where we pile dead limbs. On these cool clear nights we'll bring our lawn chairs, maybe some marshmallows, and just sit around a blazing fire built from stacked limbs.

Soon we are joined by our faithful dogs, Eddie, Ivory, and Happy. As we sit there, our faces illuminated by the firelight, Ivory puts her head on my leg, begging to be petted. If I don't pet her, she'll gently pick up my hand in her mouth and quickly put her muzzle under my hand. She likes my attention and companionship just as much as I enjoy hers.

As requested, Terry has brought his guitar. In the firelight he softly strums chords. He asks, "What do you want to hear, daddy?" "Whatever you want to play, Terry. You can't play a song I won't enjoy."

He begins playing and I sit back and just drink it in. I've noticed that as he has approached being a teenager, he's not quite as keen on doing things with me as in the past. That is a natural progression of age and is not bad in itself. However, it still brings sadness to me knowing that this age is passing quickly.

As he matures, my challenge is to find things in common that we both enjoy. One that always works is how he loves to drive my truck. He's never refused my offer of going with me so I can pull off on the side roads and let him drive. This is a trick I learned with Terry's older brothers: **Let a boy drive and he'll go anywhere with you.**

Secondly, he will stop anything to play his guitar for me. So, I request as many concerts as possible. Whether it's gentle acoustic or heart-stopping deafening electric, I enjoy hearing him play. Sometimes I ask him to join me at my drums. We have a good time just jamming. What a treat it is to play music with your son! What our neighbors hear across the field may not sound pretty, but it is wonderful for me to be with my son, playing music, and just enjoying being together.

Back at the friendship fire, Terry finishes playing and we sit there in silence. We are both comfortable sitting here quietly. In special friendships, silence says just as much as words. We enjoy each other and we both know it.

I lean back and watch the embers going up into the dark night sky. I try to see how high they glow before fading out. I breathe deeply. This time is priceless. No telephone, no TV, no interruptions.

The only noticeable noises are the sounds of the night. With the advent of spring, the crickets are chirping again. Their song carries a long way and echoes off the pine forest across our field. For probably the millionth time in my life, I thank God I live in the country.

Sitting in this "comfortable silence," I think about my friends, Henry and Nada. This sweet older couple lives in New Orleans and has helped us as volunteers each year at the camp.

About four years ago, Henry had a major stroke. Since that time he has not been able to speak or get out of bed.

Although, he is very alert and recognizes people, he just cannot express himself. He has spent these last years between hospitals, or in a special care facility.

On my last visit to New Orleans, I visited Henry and Nada at the hospital. He had recently been hospitalized due to some medical complications. All during these years since the stroke, Nada has faithfully been at his side. Her commitment of true love is always wonderful to behold. I expected a sad and emotional visit. But the joy I saw in each of their faces as they looked at each other was beyond description.

Our visit was wonderful. During our time together, Nada gave me a great gift through an insight she shared, "Curt, we often think we have to say words to tell someone we love them. But I've found this is not true. During these past years, Henry and I have found that lovers do not need words. In our own way we tell each other 'I love you' a hundred different ways daily. Many times I'll just sit here beside Henry's bed and we'll simply spend the day looking into each other's eyes."

Then Nada added a statement that was as strong as any words I've ever heard,

"I'm so thankful God has given us this special time together. It's allowed me to be deeper in love with Henry than ever before."

There was a long silence in the room after Nada finished, interrupted only by the ticking of the wall clock. She'd said what was on her heart. Henry couldn't verbally speak, although I firmly believe he heard every word Nada had just spoken. I knew by the look in his eyes that he'd fallen deeper in love with this woman he'd loved for a lifetime.

As Nada looked lovingly at Henry, I didn't say a word either because silence is the best response when you are in the presence of greatness and grace. The ensuing silence, broken only by the clock, didn't bother any of the three of us at all.

Recalling my visit to Henry and Nada, my eyes drift back to the friendship fire and the silence surrounding Terry and I as we both enjoy the warmth of the fire and the warmth of being with someone you love. Terry pokes the fire with a stick. The wind shifts and blows the smoke toward where we are sitting. After moving our lawn chairs away from the smoke, I think about one of my favorite stories concerning sitting around a fire.

When Terry's older brothers, Clint and Clay were six and eight-years-old respectively, we went on a hiking trip to the Ouachita Trail in Arkansas. We hiked about twenty-five miles through the beautiful mountains and along the Kiamichi River. On our third and last night out, we camped along a small stream. We built a good fire to warm us as the cool mountain air settled in around us.

As we cooked our supper, we were soon joined by another guest- a small mouse. He wasn't shy in the least and it was evident that he always greeted each camper here and happily shared their meal at this well-used campsite. We stacked more dead limbs on the fire and watched the surrounding mountains and forest darken around us. It's hard to describe the "wonderful lonely" feeling of camping in the deep woods miles from civilization. It is wonderful because the shackles of our busy lives are loosened. However, it is also lonely, eerie, exhilarating, and scary- all at the same time.

As the fire warmed and comforted us, out mouse friend enjoyed leftover pieces of our macaroni supper. As we sat there and just enjoyed the sounds of the night, I looked over at the boys. Clint, who was age six at this time, caught my attention. He was staring deeply into the fire. The reflection of the flames lit his face and in the corner of his eyes I saw tears welling up. I quickly recognized what he was feeling, because I've felt it many times myself when deep in the woods at dusk.

I quietly asked, "Clint, what are you thinking about?"

He sighed and stared blankly into the fire, then blurted out, "I wonder what the dogs are doing back home?"

With that, a tear trickled down one cheek. Moving over by him, I put my arm around him and said, "I don't know what they're doing right now, but I'll sure be glad to see them tomorrow night, won't you?" The three of us all sat silently staring into the comforting fire, full of macaroni, good memories, and a good dose of homesickness.

I still tell Clint's famous, "I wonder what the dogs are doing?" story. Even though he is now eighteen, we still pick at him about it. It's hard to believe it's been a dozen years since that trip.

Back at tonight's friendship fire in our back yard, Terry breaks the human silence and my reflections with his usual statement, "Well, Daddy what do you want to talk about?" I smile and look into the fire. "Oh, it doesn't matter. What would you like to talk about?" Invariably we talk about the usual things: school, baseball, recess, God, music, the stars, our dogs...

At the sound of our voices after this period of silence, Ivory thumps her massive tail on the ground in a rhythm that is similar to the crickets as they chirp. Eddie, our rat Terrier, jumps up, and barks into the darkness to remind us that he is guarding our camp fire. Happy puts his head against my leg as a reminder that he wants to be petted, too.

It is a special time around the friendship fire. After roasting marshmallows, we reluctantly return to the world of homework, electricity, and television. As we grope our way toward the back porch, Terry lets me put my arm around his shoulder. The thought hits me on how soon a boy becomes a teenager, and then although they love you no less, they don't want your hand on their shoulder, and they politely decline your invitation to sit at a friendship fire. When those years come, it'll probably just be me and the dogs out here. Nevertheless, for now, I just believe we'll build a bunch of friendship fires in the coming year.

My Latest Sun is Sinking Fast

My Latest sun is sinking fast; my race is nearly run;
My strongest trials are past, my triumph is begun.
O come, angel band, Come and around me stand;
O bear me away on your snowy wings
To my immortal home;
O bear me away on your snowy wings
To my immortal home.

Well, once again I'm sitting on the front porch of the Old House. We started this journey thirty-seven stories ago in this same rocking chair. Therefore, this porch is a good place to approach the end of this book.

As I shared in the first chapter, the Old House was built by my great-great grandfather, John Wesley Wagnon. Grandpa Wagnon was born before the Civil War. Early during this war, his father left Dry Creek to join the Southern army. He never returned home because he died from typhoid fever near Opelousas, Louisiana.

This left a mother and a large family of children alone in the wild woods of this pioneer country. Nevertheless, they stayed and persevered through the tough years of Reconstruction and beyond. Later, Grandpa Wagnon married Sarah Lyles and they homesteaded 120 acres of land about one mile south of where he'd grown up. A medium-sized stream called Crooked Bayou meandered through this area. He chose a home site where the swamp turned to higher hills with sandy soil and tall longleaf pines. There, in 1892, he and his wife began building the house we know today as The Old House.

Many stories could be told about my Grandpa Wagnon. He was evidently a country man who farmed and raised livestock and never ventured more than a day's ride from his home. His favorite saying was this:

"Boys, these woods are where I was born and this is where I plan to turn up my toes."

"In Front of the Fireplace" by Bill Iles

This final story I want to share is about the day he died. On this day, June 1, 1938, as he approached death, his family gathered around and he weakly sang the song, "My Latest Sun Is Sinking Fast":

I know I'm nearing the holy ranks of friend and kindred dear,
For I brush the dew on Jordan's banks, the crossing must be near.
O come, angel band, Come and around me stand;
O bear me away on your snowy wings
To my immortal home;
O bear me away on your snowy wings
To my immortal home.

A few hours later, he died.

As a younger person, I always wondered why we sang so many songs about death and the "Great Beyond." It seemed every song at church was about the hereafter, such as "The Unclouded Day," "I'll Fly Away," or "When We All Get to Heaven." I sometimes wondered if we were so heavenly-minded, that we were not any earthly good. This preoccupation with heaven, especially from the really older folks of my childhood, puzzled me.

But one day as a young man, I came to realize one of the reasons for these older folks' fixation on heaven. Walking through the cemetery with my special friend, Mr. Frank Miller, we went to the older part of the cemetery. Standing there, he pointed out how nearly every large double tombstone was surrounded by several smaller headstones. He sadly commented, "In the old days, hardly any family escaped losing a child in either childbirth, or later due to the flu or illness." He then pointed to his generation's burial area and continued, "Even most of my brothers and friends also experienced this." Sure enough the small graves were mute testimony to how nearly every family had been touched by the grief of a child's death.

I walked away that day with a better understanding of why the older folks always called out, "Sing number 348 - 'Where We'll Never Grow Old'." They had many precious loved ones waiting on the other side- parents, friends, spouse, and yes, even precious children. No wonder they wanted to sing, think, and talk about Heaven.

Now as I drive down our local roads, I sometimes think about who lived along these stretches during my childhood. On my favorite country road, the Longville Gravel Pit Road, there is a short stretch where during my childhood the homes of Malcolm and Lelia Heard, Lawrence and Thelma Wilson, and Aunt Mary Jane Lindsey all stood. No family members live in any of these homes now. They are all gone. Different families own each place. To the generation of my boys, these old family names mean nothing, but for me they were the homes we were always welcome at, during an era when folks still visited each other.

Continuing westward along the Gravel Pit Road, I appreciate the fact how this road, once the roughest in our parish, is now partially paved. Slowing down for the bridge over the first of several crossing over Dry Creek, I look to the south. Directly in those woods, right on down the sloping hill, is where an old spring flowed out of the ground during the day when the water table was much higher and clean clear water was easily found.

Down that hill is the spot Grandpa Wagnon's parents chose as their homestead after coming from Georgia. This road I'm now driving on, the Gravel Pit Road, is probably near the exact location of the woods trail he stood on as he watched his daddy march off to the Civil War, never to return.

Later, as I drive back down my parent's road and park in the yard of the Old House, that old song echoes again:

My Latest sun is sinking fast; my race is nearly run;
My strongest trials are past, my triumph is begun.

O come, angel band, Come and around me stand;
O bear me away on your snowy wings
To my immortal home;
O bear me away on your snowy wings
To my immortal home

I've almost gained my heavenly home, my spirit loudly sings;
Thy holy ones, behold, they come! I hear the noise of wings.
And bear my longing heart to Him, who bled and died for me;
Whose blood now cleanses from all sin, and gives me victory.

O come, angel band, come and around me stand;
O bear me away on your snowy wings
To my immortal home;
O bear me away on your snowy wings
To my immortal home.

-"My Latest Sun Is Sinking Fast." J. Haskell and William B. Bradbury.

Epilogue: Wet Paint

As I end this book, I'm aware of something I've learned through this process: **You never really finish a book.** Just when you think you have it ready, along comes an idea for an addition, correction, or something else you discover that you believe could "make it better."

It has always amused me when I've attended art shows featuring the work of my Uncle Bill. More than once, as I've stood up close to one of his oil paintings, studying the detailed texture, I've had him ease up to me and whisper, "Don't get too close to that one. The paint is still wet. I stayed up all night 'touching it up.'"

I now understand why Uncle Bill kept touching up his paintings- when we step back and look at something we've "made," we can always see some way it could be improved. So please accept this book from me- even though the paint is still wet.

Make it your own and enjoy it.

During Christmas 1973, this same uncle, Bill Iles, gave me a very unusual present: a blank notebook. Little did he, or I, know this little book would be the starting line of my journey of writing. Since that Christmas three decades ago, I have filled many notebooks with my scribbling.

Many of the stories you've just read evolved from those journal entries. Many more lie buried in that precious stack of journals I keep in a cardboard box. Some stories may find their way into future books, while others are so personal I would never share them with anyone. Some are pretty good (I think.) However, when I read other entries, I say, "What in the world was he thinking when he wrote that garbage?"

The following words of encouragement come from the original letter Uncle Bill inserted in that first journal. I still cherish this simple handwritten note in his descriptive handwriting,

Curt-

I hope you use this book as if it were a silent friend– something to confide in. Write down your personal observations about the world around you. . . whether it is something specific, like the fragile mystery of a spider's lace-like web, or something general like, "All people are interesting– sometimes."

But write– don't worry about sentence structure, or spelling, or punctuation, or anything else– invent your own way of putting it down. . . but write.

Write about the things that turn you on– the things you like, and the things you love. And also write about the pain you see and feel– the things that upset you or disturb you. In writing these things down in this, your little book, you will be discovering parts of yourself that lie deep within, next to the soul of your being . . . and also discovering parts of the awesome sacred mystery of life– and the beauty of words. The more we feel (both joy and pain), the more we are alive and complete as human beings.

With my love I offer you these blank pages– fill them with your feelings.

-Love, Bill

So once again, here I sit on the front porch of the Old House. In my hands, I hold a journal full of empty pages. Again, I begin the joyful and painful task of turning the deep feelings of my heart into visible, written words.

I write for the same simple reason as when I wrote the first sentence in that original journal: I write because I enjoy it. It doesn't matter if anyone ever sees this new story I'm writing, or if it ever makes it into some future book.

I write because it brings me joy… and helps me better understand this miracle we call life.

. . . And there is no place where I experience this surrounding miracle more clearly, than when I sit here on the front porch of this house…

. . . The Old House, at the end of the road, deep in the woods on Crooked Bayou.

Curt Iles

ABOUT THE AUTHOR

Curt Iles lives in Dry Creek, Louisiana with his wife, DeDe, and their three sons.

In the stories comprising *The Old House*, Iles draws on his experiences of growing up in the rural community where his family has lived for over 150 years.

Curt Iles has worked as a teacher, coach, and school administrator. For the past ten years, he has served as director of a year - round youth camp, Dry Creek Baptist Camp.

The Old House is his second published book. His first book, *Stories from the Creekbank*, is also available from 1stBooks Library.

Contact the author at curtiles@aol.com.